Annie **Mack**

Whatta You Lookin' At?

Publishing Copyright © 2024 Cresting Wave Publishing, LLC

ISBN: 978-1-956048-99-5

Published by Cresting Wave Publishing, LLC

"You Buy a Book, We Plant a Tree!"

Edited by Kris Neely

Layout by Kris Neely and Lazar Kackarovski

Photography and Photographic Descriptions by Annie Mack

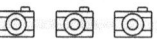

Cover Photos. Copyright © Annie Mack

Front cover left: *Ikebana*, 2020

Front cover right: *Precipice Bridge*, 2023

Back cover left: *Time and Space*, 2022

Back cover right: *Across the Universe*, 2017

CONTENTS

EDITOR'S **NOTE**

As I mentioned in her first book, it has been my pleasure to know Annie personally for 50 years — as a student, teacher, activist, author, artist — and friend. And as her friend and editor I can testify that editing her work takes a bit more time and focus — because she is trying to convey ideas, concepts, and a vision in a singular way.

As such, you'll notice that I am presenting the layout of Annie's writing in a bit freer, looser, more flowing format than one might expect in a book like this. In such a way, the cause of that conveyance is served. And you'll also notice the positioning and orientation of the pictures in this book are "different" from a traditional photography book – that's intentional. By positioning the pictures at unexpected angles or with "effects," we hope it will encourage readers to slow down and absorb the unique imagery of this artist.

Next, you may also see references to he, she, and (s)he in this work — gender identity is beautiful.

So, hang on tight because here comes Annie!

Kris Neely

Co-Founder / Senior Editor
Cresting Wave Publishing

INTRODUCTION

ONCE UPON A TIME IN THE LASCAUX CAVE

I am not a photographer. Let's settle that right now.

I don't do weddings or events, make studio appointments, or sell wallet prints.

I am an artist, and I make art with photographic equipment.

I create images that don't look or act like photos, and I am denied admittance to many competitions, galleries, and photo shows all the time.

Why?

Because many judges/spectators don't appreciate 'What They're Looking At.'

I can explain.

I am sure — beyond even the most unreasonable doubt — that the first artist, likely a caveman with a hunk of charcoal, upon drawing something, *anything* on a cave wall, was instantly asked, "What *is* it?"

Understandable. Cave walls and charcoal not being too user-friendly, fair question.

Moreover, nobody (*NOBODY!*) had ever seen anything like it, with the "it" depicting a real object on a different medium. And the viewer didn't really mean "what" is it (charcoal on rock, Ya eedjit.) (S)he meant "What's it *supposed* to be?"

And so, the first misunderstood artist was born.[1]

---

1   And with it, the first need for a double martini with two olives, extra dry, and keep 'em coming...

So ... let's try to understand *What U Lookin' At?*

Most of the pieces in this book are abstract photography. It's easier to show than tell, but in a nutshell:

- Abstraction is a reduction of an image to its essential elements.

- Painters or sculptors create abstracts by obscuring or illuminating details while retaining the core geometrics or an evocative, definitive color or pattern that *suggests* the original.

- Abstract photographers seek out shots that are more than their face value. Shapes, shadows, or hues that *remind* the viewer of a scene, an emotional moment, or an unseen concept like love, justice, or joy.

- Think of brands or logos, the Nike swish, the Pepsi yin/yang, the Olympics five color interlocking circles.

- These images are clearly not "the thing" but are *symbolic* of the product or event.

  o The swoosh is action — movement, speed, sports.

  o The Yin/Yang is not the drink — but the sense of balance and pleasure *from* the drinking.

  o The colored circles represent — rings, as rewards or laurels, the interconnectedness of all humans, and the "Circle of Life" — which is the infinite.

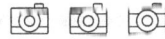

So, to appreciate abstractions, look at the image.

In your mind, break it down to the bare bones.

Then, ask yourself if you "feel it." It might be ... anything.

Or any thing.

Images that make you "feel" them. No need for words or even recognizable reality. Like the Zen idea of "satori" – you "get it" without intellectual analysis, language, or opinion.

You just "feel it."

Abstract photographic images lie somewhere between technically precise reproductions and "fling pixels and see where they land." So, in the language of the 2024 street, abstractionists are considered "kinda suss" by some museums, galleries, competitions, or commercial art enterprises.

Abstractionists are not invited to photo shows. They tell us: "Your [*insert word that more-or-less means "stuff" here*] does not fit our categories: landscapes, portraits, photojournalism, etc. We're bounced from "art" shows. "You people are machinists, not painters / not sculptors / not "real" artists."

Heard it all. Hear it often. Try to absorb and chill.

We are outliers, and we are cool with that.

Our creative journeys are more freeform than the quests of artists who work in specific disciplines. I'm a member of a tribe (Abstract Photographers International) on Instagram that Zoom-meets regularly to show our latest images ... inventions ... art ... and to take and give constructive feedback.

Most of us make "found art."

We are looking for this art as we stroll around the nabe, hoping to spy something intriguing: a splatter of paint, a cluster of shadow-shapes, the visual effects of nature (or man), or an unusual texture. The mind, unbidden, knows it when it sees it. Like the definition of obscenity: we can't tell you *what* we're seeking, but we know it *when* we see it!

And we do this pretty much as loners. Solitary wanderers seeking surprise discoveries.

Like Columbus sailing the ocean blue. On paper, "Trying to get to India," but in reality, more like Getting out of the country on the King's dime and floating around until he/they blundered into an enormous, unknown continent. ("Who knew?! Uh...yeah, meant to do that!")

Abstract denizens go looking to see .. just what's ... out there. It's a journey of imagination rather than of destination. Seeking the Found. As Rod Serling of Twilight Zone fame said: "Imagination... its limits are only those of the mind itself."

By contrast, the people of traditional camera work may enact a "photo shoot." To wit...

- A professional photographer advertises trips to well-known pretty places - mountains, waterfalls, deserts (reliably there and not too changeable), architectural treasures such as downtown Paris, red barns in wheat fields, or quaint harbors.

- Folks and their equipment are piled into group transport.

- And upon arrival, they haul out the apparatus and start snapping.

- The takeaway: the participant folks have "an experience," and the leader introduces techniques, assists with balky gear, and referees one-upmanship contests of camera-setting minutiae, brand preference, or "The Shot That Got Away."

These trips are usually fun and informational; the group members bond and the lucky ones may remain pals for many years afterward.

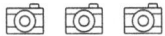

On the other hand, a "photo shoot" with abstractionists is an entirely different animal. For example:

- We might meet at the local "Pick-n-Pull" (or whatever is the vernacular for the junkyard/auto wreckers in your locale.)
  - We each cough up five bucks or so to poke around the "exhibits/sights" (read: rubbish.)

- Or, we alert our comrades, by any means possible, to a new cluster of bando / rusty / savaged shipping containers down at the railyards.

- Or, we head downtown to a construction/renovation site to check out those plywood-and-chain-link barriers slathered with stickers, graffiti, and impotent warnings against posting handbills.

- Or, we see a building being demolished and *run like the wind* to the dumpsters! These are the absolute GOLD MINES of abstract photographers. Especially if they've been burnt (actually, that puts them into Platinum or Diamond-mine status.)[2]

Bottom line: we find exquisite beauty or stark design in ... cracked antique auto glass ... melted or gouged paints... in graffiti ... or advanced decay.

We get dirty and talk dirty. We tumble into containers ... snag our jeans on barbed wire and rusty fenders ... step into puddles of goosh, or ... worse ... and cuss (in several dialects!) And we develop cunning Spidey senses and plausible cover stories to avoid arrest for trespassing.

In the end, abstractionists bond over scars, quick escapes, and other horror stories and are initiated as blood brothers and sanguinity sisters for life! It's a lifestyle.

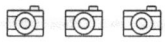

---

2   FYI, we don't start the fires. We do NOT encourage others to start fires, either. We just find the fantastically splendid burnt stuff and make art.

WHATTA U LOOKIN AT:
SO, WHAT?

The Whatta, First Step: Literally, what is actually there?

Anything vaguely recognizable? Identify colors, geometrics, texture(s) … without speculation or imagination.

Be the Lascaux Cave artist/caveman we discussed earlier…

First, scope out the basics…

See.

Observe.

Notice.

… without speculation or imagination.

Then, be the caveman's pal and exhibit the curious mind looking for meaning.

Here's how to do both — with abstracts and more traditional genres.

In Realism, i.e., representational art, the "What" is …Duh Obvious:

The breathtaking landscape

The serenely beautiful woman

Dogs of familiar breeds, seated around a table, playing poker and drinking beer

You are transported to specific coordinates in time and space and see every detail...

Half Dome covered in snow

The mysterious smile

The ace of clubs held in a dog's paw, skillfully rendered by an artist

You know what it is supposed to be right off the bat. Even if there are glaring flaws (seriously, a bulldog could never keep a cigar in his teeth at that impossible angle), there is reference to a level of "factiness" therein.

But in abstract art — not so much.

Blocks of color

Irregular shapes

Odd textures

... and better yet, Untitled (No cue from the artist!)

What? Just show me "what" you want me to see, and I'm on to the next one. Aaaand there's the gotcha. "What" just *ain't.*

The Big Picture (*yes, I know what I did there),* the subject of an abstract probably doesn't exist, *per se,* in real life. The artist snatches globs of 'visual' and wills it into being: a poem, a slap in the face, an intangible quality, or something as gossamer as the merest fleeting sensation.

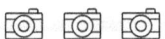

It's a concept or ideal, not...

The Real Thing

Though the art is real stuff (charcoal on rock … paint on canvas … ink on paper), it jumps the chasm from the everyday world into imagination, where What can be … anything.

A pure abstract is pretty much all form and little function, and it messes with every norm about what an image is "supposed" to be.

One of my favorite photo quotes is from David Alan Harvey:

"I don't shoot what it looks like; I shoot what it feels like."

Another quote (*unattributed so far*) says:

"You aren't doing it wrong if no one knows what you're doing."

Disclosure: **half the time**…

I.really.don't.know.what.I'm.doing.

I capture light and shadow in my magic box, download it, and futz around with wizardly tools, and am astonished when I discover a vision I hadn't been looking for, much less intentionally composing.

Sometimes, I dazzle myself.

Sometimes, I want to sweep everything off the work table and smash the printer.

Most times (as printers and worktables are expensive and artists are usually broke), I maintain enough good sense to refrain from going all Hulk, and I show the image I'm working on to another abstractionist.

And, *voila*, (s)he see *all sorts* of fantastic stuff that I simply *had.not.seen.*

To be fair, they often don't know what I had seen either. But, to quote the great Miles Davis from his illuminating 1959 album *Kind of Blue*, "So What?"

The miracle of Art is that it opens our eyes to glorious other worlds…

What ... is ... what ... you ... make ... it!

Context is distorted or removed in the most extreme abstracts, leaving everyone adrift in a miraculous state of the human mind: a sea of possibilities. This state can be exhilarating or terrifying, depending on how adventurous or anal the viewer is.

But as every Zen master since Buddha has tried to tell us, when boundaries, comfort zones, norms, and "normal" are swept away, some viewers are afraid they won't get the "right" answer.

Breaking News: Art is not *Jeopardy!*

Real Right Answer: There is no *right* answer.

There is *your* answer.

Whatever the image does ... for you.

And that's correct.

Abstract artists do what they must do and then turn the beast loose in the world, where it takes on a life of its own, and there's no calling it back.

If that didn't scare the crap out of you, then come and play!

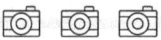

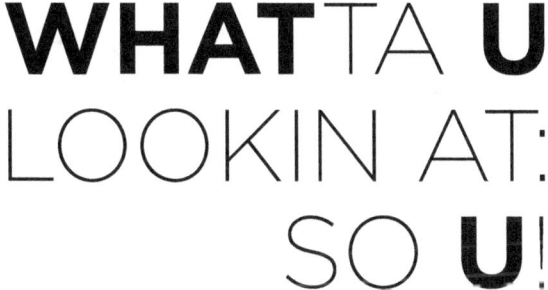

WHATTA U LOOKIN AT: SO U!

A rt is self-expression. So, (looking up at this chapter heading above) the **What**, and one of the **U**'s, is the Artist.

Bob Dylan, artist extraordinaire on many levels, said, "All I can do is be me... whoever that is."[3] If you think you need to "get" an artist's work, find out about the artist as a person.

No artist lives or works in a vacuum but creates in The Now[4]. She is organically influenced by the worlds swirling around her: geography, culture, religion (or lack thereof), life experiences, and her personal story, just to name a few.

We love to think we're unique, special, one-of-a-kind, and all that. Naah! We are *so* mirrors of our environments. The artist bumps into comfortable themes or elements that she revisits, collects ideas, concepts, and imagery, and creates her Visual Vocabulary (aka Shape Vocabulary, her Personal Symbology.) Some of this may be personal and cryptic in the extreme.

---

3   Interview with the *New York Times*, 1965.
4   Edna Mode, *The Incredibles*, Disney Pictures, 2004.

We've all read Artist Statements at galleries. Some artists are accessible and secure in their artiness. Others are obscure, aloof, condescending, and even pretentious, ("You ... wouldn't understand.") Whatever they offer, I promise you can deal.

The point is that as a viewer if you like her work, you don't need to comprehend fully or agree to appreciate what the artist does or says.

You like her art.

For itself.

Not for her or who she is.

But for what her self-expression conveys to you.

More help: Find out what's been done by... well ... *everybody*.

Learning art history makes you a better artist (reinventing the wheel is a waste of energy) and shows that many people do the same things at the same time. Widespread Zeitgeists, geographically or socially significant disruptions, or other lesser local milieu almost always influence the artists and provoke similar reactions among them. Archetypes and emotional touchstones (ubiquitous themes or symbols) are rampant across the universe. "Art is theft," Pablo Picasso told us[5], so creativity isn't plagiarism (i.e., stealing) unless you execute a full-on heist and rip off a significant chunk of physical or intellectual property. Technically, it's hard to say anything is original, so seeing a popular element or allusion to a current "thing" is inevitable.

Again, it can also help to research the artist's works. Since the creative's raison d'etre is to make a statement or express a truth, find out where he or she was in real space or personal development. Dig around for any writing or speaking she/he might have done. You can also learn about the person's impact by the rotten tomatoes, glowing praise, piercing snark, and other reactions tossed at her by bloggers, reviewers, and commentators. Plenty of that out there. And an excellent opportunity to practice evaluating and validating sources.

---

5   Quoted in *Steal Like an Artist:10 Things Nobody Told You About Being Creative.* Austin Kleon, 2012, Workman Publishing Company, Inc., NY, NY. A book every artist should have.

When all else fails, ask or listen. I showed up to hear a talk by an artist, Julia, who works in assemblage with textiles and odd objects. There was yarn, wire, magic marker, and crumpled paper all over the place, and I wasn't sure What was happening.

Her explanation: she'd ripped pieces out of art magazines and fliers to protest the lack of inclusion and discrimination against female-identifying artists. On a poster, she blacked out the names of the dozen males in a show and highlighted the lucky one or two females invited. She attached a miniature fabric skirt over a photo of a man heaving paint at a canvas, which is muscular and macho and OK for guys but is snorted at when women try it (ask any female artist; this is Truth.)

Light Bulb Goes On! Julia had handed us a little key, and suddenly, her art and its trenchant message were wide open.[6] And, since I wasn't worrying about what I might've missed, I enjoyed her works according to her purpose and my sensibilities.

As it should be!

📷 📷 📷

The next, and a very important **U,** is You. What do *you* see in the image? Why does it resonate with *you*? Remember that Rorschach inkblot test from Psych 101? *"Look at this picture. What might it be?"* The good doctor was counting on the human mind's strong tendency to "Find Meaning" in an ambiguous image. It's called "pareidolia." a word to describe the urge to parse out human faces in tree bark, a letter of the alphabet in an unrelated object, Jesus on a piece of toast — you get it.

Like the Rorschach, **WHAT-YOU-SEE** gives insights into your values, experience, psyche, and possible neuroses.

---

6   Julia Couzens, American artist, March 10, 2023, speaking at John Natsoulas Gallery, Davis, CA.

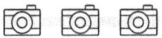

Maybe this is why viewing abstracts is uncomfortable for some folks...they're looking into, for lack of a better word, a mirror and discovering the Man in There: Uh, oh, or Oh Wow!

WHEN TO EXPLAIN

Art is to be experienced, absorbed, and...*OK, <u>sometimes</u>* dissected. But not to the point of atomization.

I believe that the most memorable art you see will yank you off your feet and into the frame. Or lure you with an insidious hook that slowly reels you in. And you won't even notice or care if there is a label or a blurb.

IFKYK.

It's like a joke. You don't slowly begin to realize a joke over time. You hear it and get it in a flash — like a *thunderclap*. You appreciate the art. Nonetheless, the art community buzzes with discussion of whether or not to title a work or include expository prose. This argument NEVER goes away.

I think more painters and sculptors get away with "untitled" or dissertation-length labels with shi*loads of obfuscation because everyone knows it's Paint, Clay, or Stone, and they're making it look like ... something else.

Photography is just light recorded on a medium, but it is expected to be a real scene or an actual object, not "art" or "Art." And back to the old *Right Answer Theory*: there isn't one; the one you think is right is right. Only artists have the privilege to attach or not to attach signage, monikers, or indicators.

In any case, I think the creator should avoid wasting energy by insisting that her explanation is the only one and let viewers "complete the image"[7] with their ideas or feelings about a piece, which are totally legit. Beauty is in the mind of the beholder.

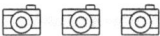

Best Answer: Look first at the art and last at the title. (My publishers, Laura and Kris, set up the page progression of my books for this. Nice.)

---

7   Jeff Koons, American artist, from a segment of *60 Minutes*, CBS, aired on 5/21/2023.

the other hand, work externally. No need for *us* to go rummaging around in our psyches for inspiration or subject matter! Just get out of the house and into the world of light, color, action, fests, and stimulating venues. Plus, photo equipment is bossy-automatic and will drag us ahead by the nose if we can't think of anything. If we don't have a specific shot in mind, we are rarely disappointed with whatever crosses our paths. We go looking to find things that we don't own and aren't responsible for and make art out of them! Creators seek the release of inner turmoil. Hunters capture the wild life!

8. **Believe in yourself and your work**. Believe me, at times, it seems like you're the only one who does. Don't despair or surrender. The kid in *The Polar Express* finally believed and he heard that beautiful little bell for a lifetime.

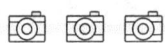

BASIC "SUGGESTIONS,"
"GUIDELINES," & "IMHOS"

OK, so having argued so convincingly against explanation, I still have just a few little "suggestions" or "guidelines," "just sayin''s," or whatever.

Take 'em or leave 'em. Either way, I'm cool.

1. **Focus**. The Camera. Blurred lines are fine for Robin Thicke, and alternate realities are fine subjects for abstractionists. But keep your edge! Fuzzy, indistinct images are for sappy greeting cards. This is art, not a Hallmark moment...

2. **KISS** (yes, that old reliable): **Keep It Simple Stupid**). It's a good idea, no matter how musty. Abstracts are supposed to be reductions to essential elements. If they get too busy or fussy, your message gets muddled. Also, **KISS** your titles. Treat them like haiku — short, concentrated, and evocative. Bonus Points: a single word with multiple meanings or nuances.

3. **Practice composition.** Simple geometrics (polygons, circles, lines) are great starting points. They can be dominant or hinted at. In any case, they establish a foothold and lend stability. Unity, Balance, and Proportion are good concepts to remember, whether mind-blowing or rule-breaking. Excitement is fantastic; a hot mess is not.

4. **Learn color theory**. Everything doesn't have to *match*, but it should *interact* somehow. One good rule of thumb (especially when making photos with rust, paint, and other man-made decay): three colors minimum and not too much more (two shades of one color is OK) — and have at least one color in noticeable contrast to the others. This kicks it up a notch!

5. **Study the Elements and Principles of Design**. In general, Elements are line, shape, value, color, movement, size, and pattern. Principles are harmony, contrast, rhythm, repetition, gradation, balance, and dominance. Go look them up, I'm on a word limit. Please don't carry around the list and tick off every box per composition. *Less is More!* Trust your intuition. Get familiar with these through osmosis; as you shoot, they will surface. Even better: in processing, they'll help you find that missing piece that sparks it all and gives it some oomph.

6. **Be prepared**. If you exhibit online or in person, you're gonna hear it. That second caveman will show up right away. Prepare varied responses to "What IS it?" Reading the inflection is key. If the viewer is wondrously curious and amazed, be grateful and gracious. If they're sneering, take a breath and dig up an appropriate script. Short and witty is good, and it is handy to turn the question around to the viewer ("What do you see in it?") for a moment. Sometimes, a curious look or teensy raised eyebrow will suffice. Also, don't drive off patrons with excruciating personal revelations (*TMI! TMI!*). Don't get all salty if they say, "Oh look! It's a horse!" when you were *clearly* depicting "Deep Emotions Locked in Blackened Time."[8] And get ready to absorb rudeness, ignorance, or condescension. "My five-year-old could've done that!" is best shrugged off, although The Invisible Thought Bubble is snarking loudly, "Well, why doesn't he, and make you rich?" Enjoy a second with that little voice, but I recommend keeping it to yourself. Just smile without teeth and excuse yourself over to the *hors d'oeuvres* (which you probably brought to this reception) and get busy with a gooey cupcake or other noshes that demand your full attention.

7. **Have fun!** If it isn't fun, why bother? Art doesn't have to be dead serious all the time. I listen to painters or sculptors talk about their process, and far too often, I hear tales of anxiety and creative paralysis. Angst at baring their innermost feelings on a canvas! Anecdotes of "...the hard place I was going through at the time." Dark pools of personal struggles from which art has been dredged! Photographers, on

---

8   Deep Emotions Locked in Blackened Time. I googled Pretentious Titles and was directed to a website that's been defunct for 15 years and everyone used fake names and if you click on it your computer will be destroyed by a virus. This is the best accreditation I can do.

A FEW HOW-TO'S:
MACRO PHOTOGRAPHY,
LAYERING, & ICM

MACRO PHOTOGRAPHY

Macro is extreme short-range shooting, either with special lenses or by crowding into the very *up-close-and-personal* space of a large object and cropping it like crazy. What's happened is that the context is taken away or skewed, the proportion is all out of whack, and everything is cast loose from its moorings to leave just the essence of the photograph.

Another more visual example – a grasshopper on the car windshield is now an enormous mutant monster terrorizing the roadway. AKA "forced perspective."

And hugely entertaining.

Less weird but more intriguing example: Margrethe Mather (1885-1952) made a close-up shot of the midriff/stomach of an androgynous person wearing a gi or kimono, who is lifting apart the folds of the garment. The image was meticulously arranged to eliminate gender clues like body hair, size of hands, traditional male-female attire or presentation.

It's compelling because — it.makes.you.look.

It seems simple at first glance — and it's anything but.

One more example: a narrow focus view of a complicated machine, to the point that a gizmo, flange, or other strange whatchamacallit is so removed from the big picture that it appears otherworldly. Viewer (either silently or explosively verbal, turning head at a diagonal, squinting): "What the *HELL* is that?"

LAYERING

Layering is a type of multiple exposure, recently made exponentially easier by computer technology. All those hours of dodging, burning, and sloshing around in darkroom developer tanks (anyone younger than 25: "*What?*") are now matched by any foo who can click a mouse and plunk one image over another.

Yeah, well, just because it's easy doesn't necessarily make it good. Creating something artful still requires talent and an eye for composition.

Some seriously advanced cameras can juggle all that stuff inside, and Photoshop has a few tricks up the sleeve that are more or less magic (just trust, don't ask). The trick is to find a blend without venturing beyond "interesting" or "curious" to "bollixed[9]."

In short, reality and fantasy can really go at it. Often classified as "mixed media" in photo contests or shows because it's not a "straight shot," call it what you want; it can be awesome.

ICM = INTENTIONAL CAMERA MOVEMENT

I have tried to be open-minded, curious, or at least tolerant, but I'm just not a big fan.

ICM is trending at the moment and has been around forever, but IMHO, it's predictable and gimmicky. When novices try ICM by jiggling the camera in front of a recognizable human

---

9   The American English term for this is usually censored. You get the gist.

or landmark, it comes out looking like a tourist's snapshot (... *why not cut off the person's head while you're at it?*). These images emerge like those mysterious fumble-bloopers that pop up in your phone without your knowledge or consent.

You can mean to do that, and sometimes a lucky accident makes a cool shot, but shaking the lens as a regular practice doesn't make especially compelling or original art.

All that said, *if it's done well*, ICM can be freakin awesome.

At its finest, it can be "painterly," *i.e.* resembling the hand-made strokes of a brush or pen. The most effective ICMs use movement to imply emotional stirring or potential energy rather than the simple recording of physics, such as the light trail of a powerful locomotive, a speeding bullet, or a flying superhero, all of which have been done ad infinitum.

If you want to see *absolutely badass* ICM, look up my IG tribe members in the acknowledgments; they are grandmasters in this field. However, most of their truly spectacular works use ICM *together* with several other processing tools to avoid an amateurish result. The best use of ICM (repeat: IMHO) is ... sparingly.

I use it rarely, if at all, so you won't see much here. *OK, Let's get LOOKIN!*

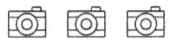

OUTLINE OF
PHOTOS

DUMPSTERS!

- Origen
- Brink
- How The Light Gets In
- Hieroglyph Bird
- Aqua Lilac

SAME TIME, PLACE...

- Tugboat
- Marsh & Moon
- Monochrome
- Burnt Red Monochrome

FIGURES

- Inuit
- Tall Woman
- Swimsuit
- Dance In Rehearsal
- Kiss Me (Hot)
- Walkin In The Hood

MULTIPLE EXPOSURE

- Japanese Garden W Trees
- Cosmic Travel
- Cosmic Tunnel
- Water Hole At Evening
- Water Hole In Heat Of Afternoon
- Colors Of Music
- Guitarra

PAINT NOT PAINTING

- Uphill Both Ways
- Boy At The Dike
- Nightfall
- The Fish That Got Away
- Kiss Me
- Sabbath Candle
- Cabin In The Woods
- Walking In Winter Woods
- Sax
- Fledgling
- Beach At Sunset

Editor's Note: A reminder, please. I've purposely positioned many of the pictures on the following pages in locations that are anything but "centered" on the page. This is done purposely because the human eye looks at any page from the center out, and I want readers to "encounter" this art and not become numb to it because of an "always centered" placement. Also, you'll see the art on the right-hand page; its description will be at the bottom of the left-hand page opposite.

Thanks!

Kris Neely

DUMPSTERS!

A<small>ND OTHER METAL DISASTERS.</small>
T<small>HE</small> A<small>BSTRACTIONISTS'</small> F<small>IELD</small> T<small>RIP!</small>

01

ORIGEN (2021)

From a burnt metal dumpster.
The Object Selection tool in Photoshop cut around all the tight stuff and plopped it onto a jet-black background.
Way ... cool!

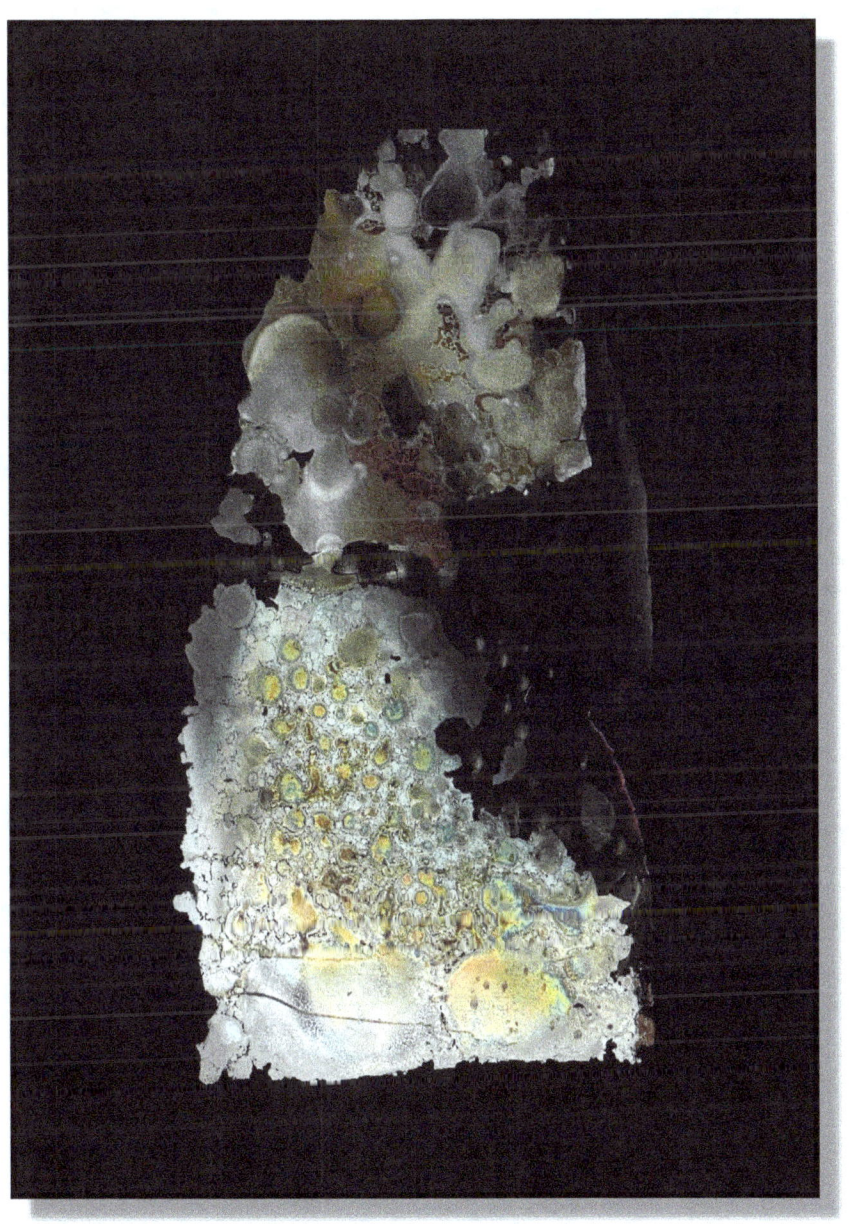

02

BRINK (2020)

Viewers have suggested ice, abyss, river, sinkhole, a close-up of a melting ice shelf, and a white marble crypt.

What *you* see — is what *you* get.

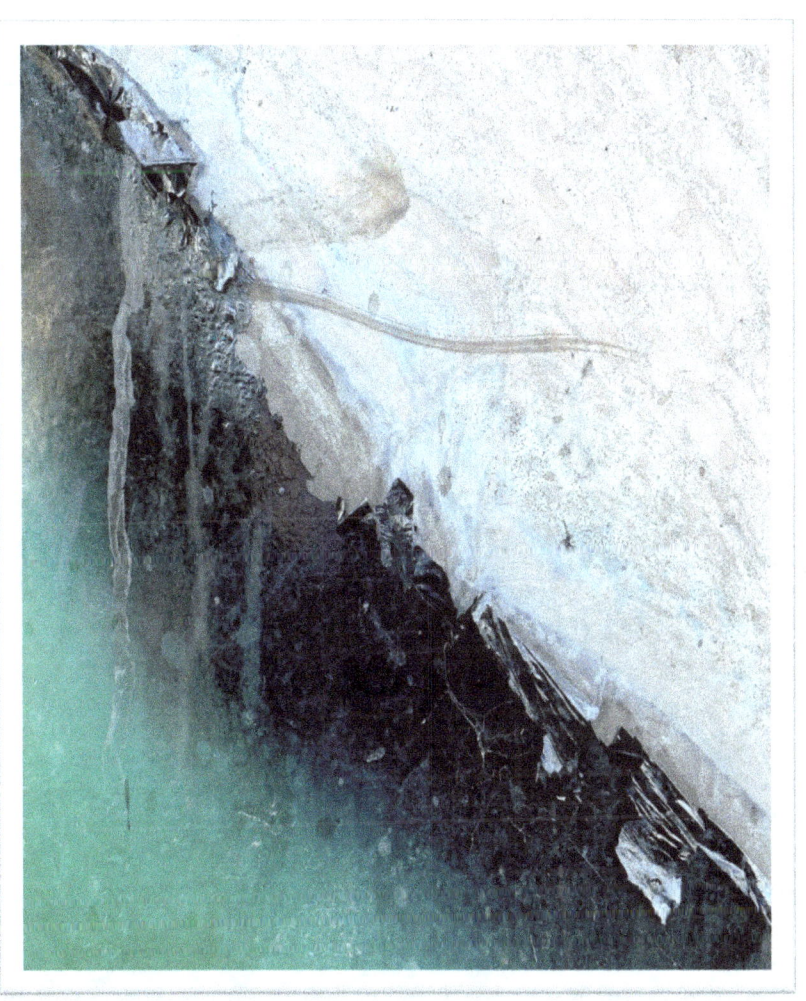

03

HOW THE LIGHT GETS IN (2019)

A near-ancient pickup truck (1950s or so)
pays homage to ... Leonard Cohen.

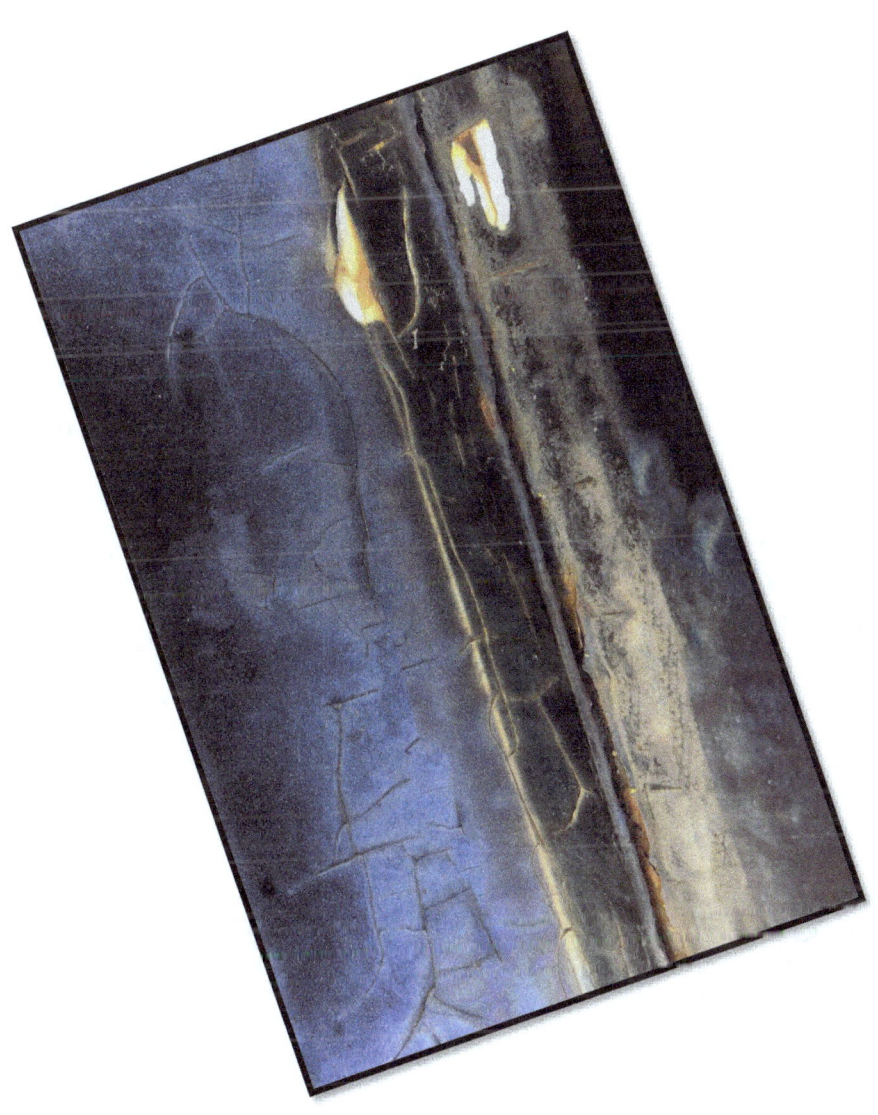

04

HIEROGLYPH BIRD (2018)

Or the Grim Reaper giving you the side eye.

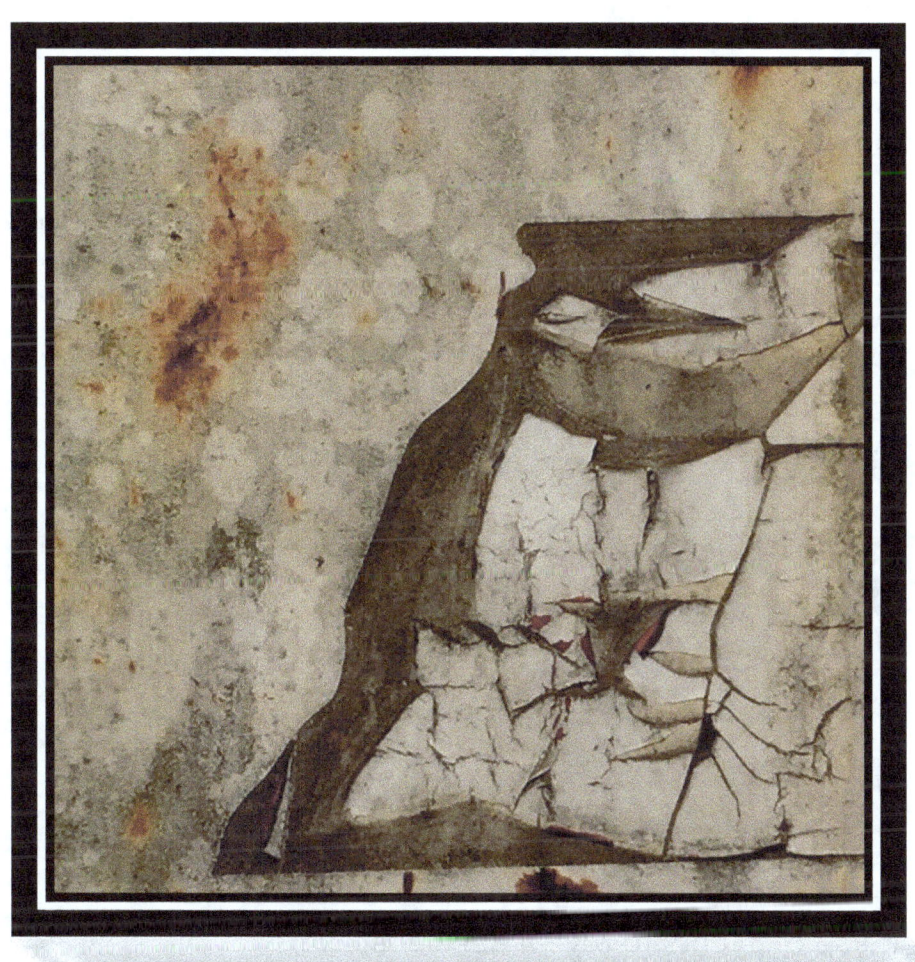

05

AQUA LILAC (2020)

A shipping container.

They are repainted regularly, then scratched
and gouged in the course of events to reveal delicious layers.

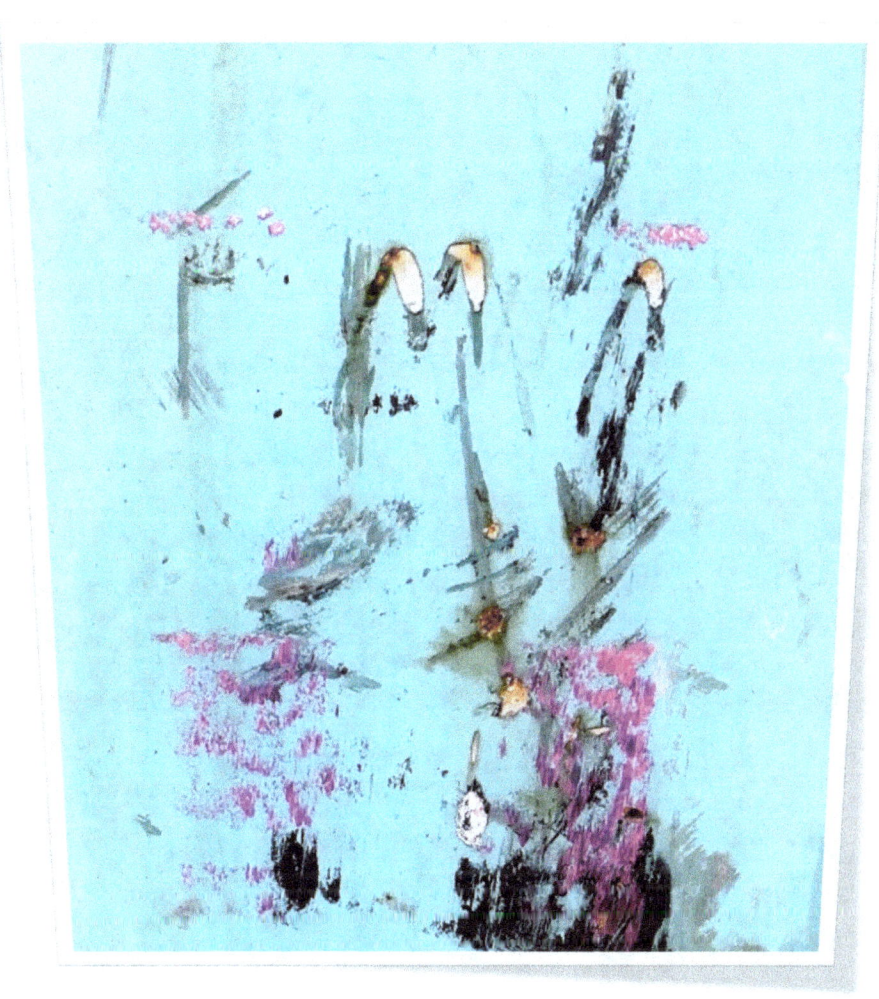

SAME TIME, PLACE

Tugboat and *Marsh & Moon* were parts of an artist's homemade worktable, with minimal photo processing.

I think the woodiness evokes the weathering of piers and boat docks.

The *Monochromes* were found on a galvanized metal light pole, used with various adhesive tapes as a message center.

06

TUGBOAT (2020)

Can you hear the foghorn?

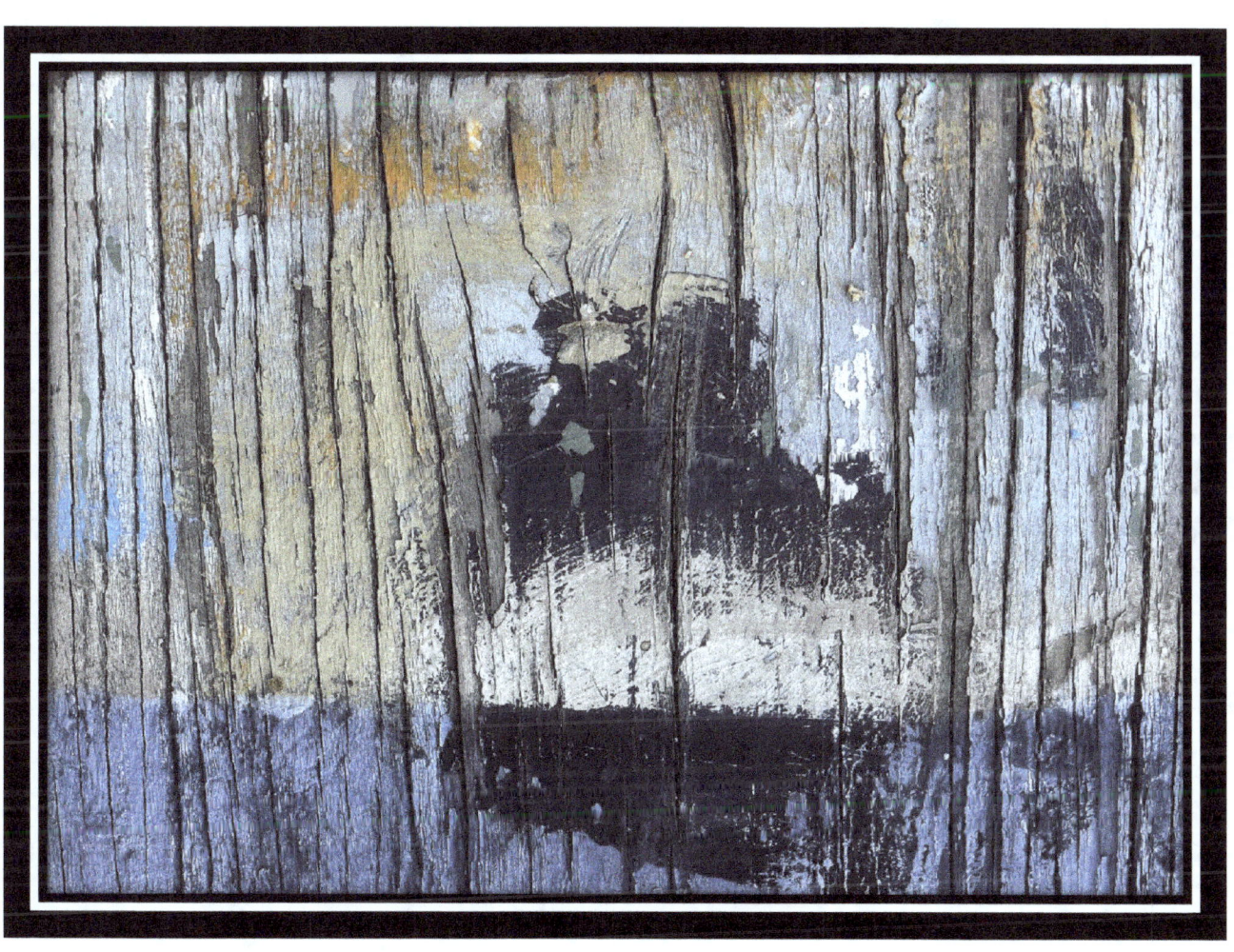

07

MARSH AND MOON (2020)

Decaying wood presents like a screen of spindly saplings.

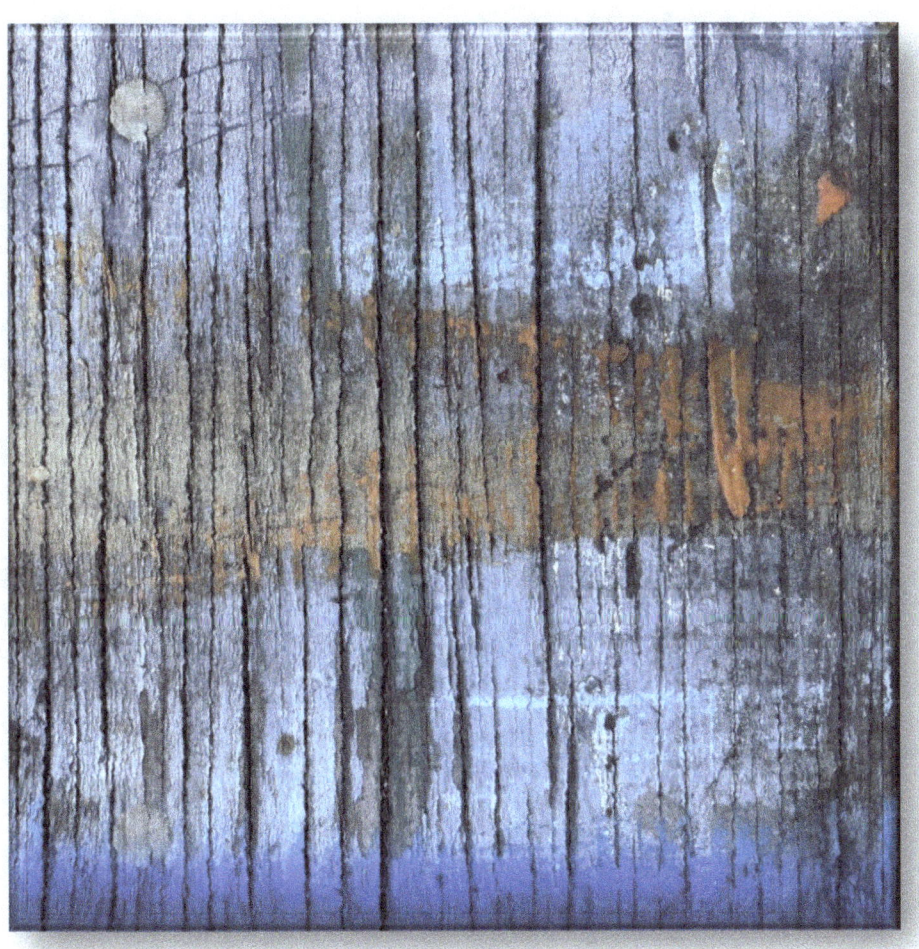

08

MONOCHROME (2021)

I imagine the industrial zone on the city's outskirts.

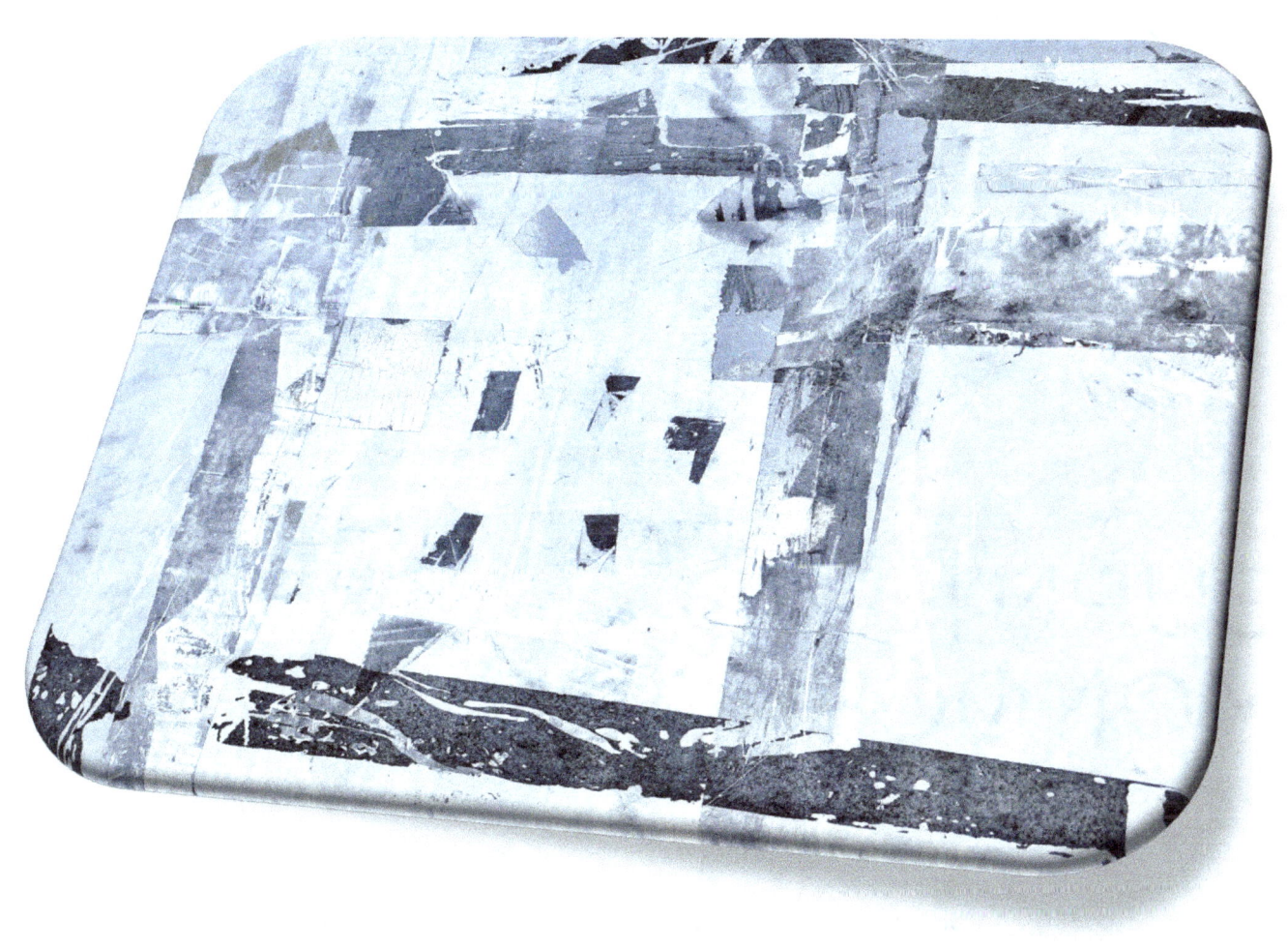

09

BURNT RED MONOCHROME (2021)

But now it's a concert poster, or a painted-over window, or....or... a...

FIGURES

Pareidolia IS THE HUMAN URGE TO SEE FACES

OR OTHER HUMAN FEATURES IN NATURE OR INANIMATE OBJECTS.

10

INUIT (2020)

A personal favorite. Weather-beaten adhesive tape on galvanized metal.

The cold colors evoked endless snow and ice.
The man inside the parka is incomplete ... ... as if the harsh elements...
... were chiseling... ... his flesh... ... closer to the... ... bone.

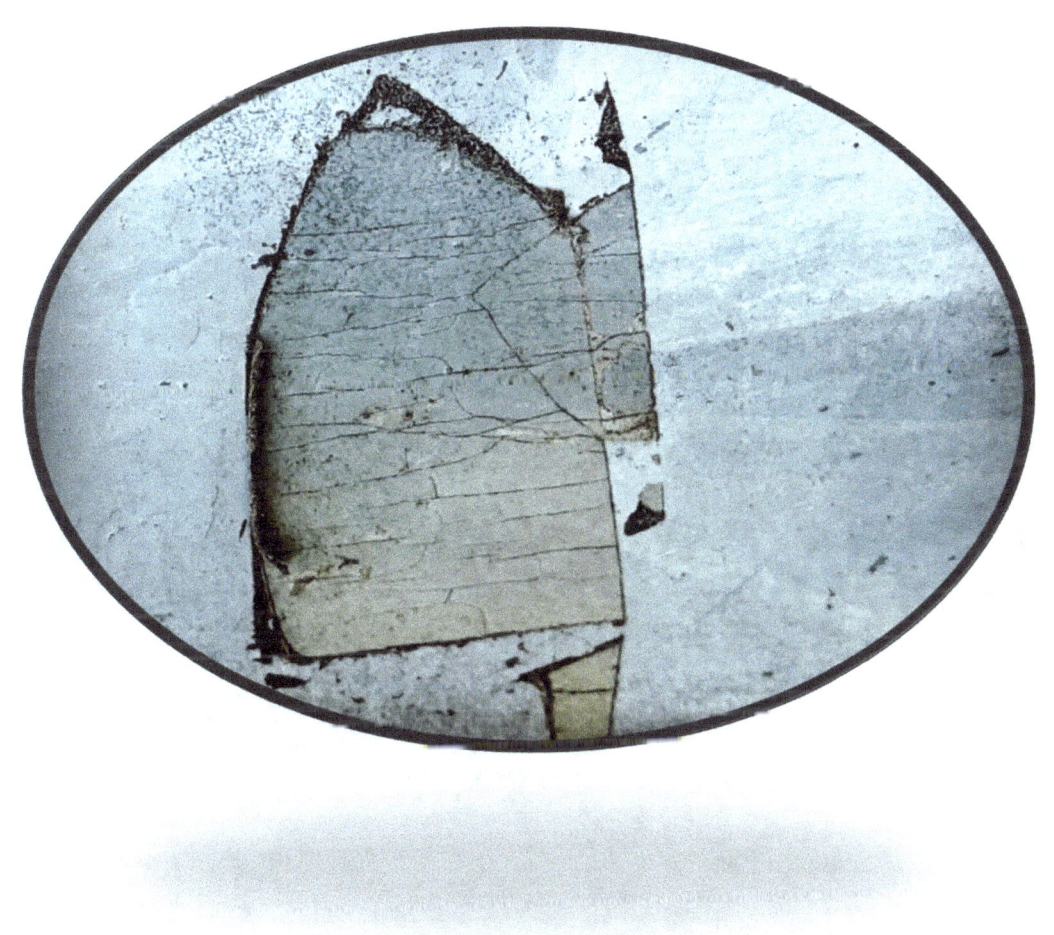

11

TALL WOMAN (2020)

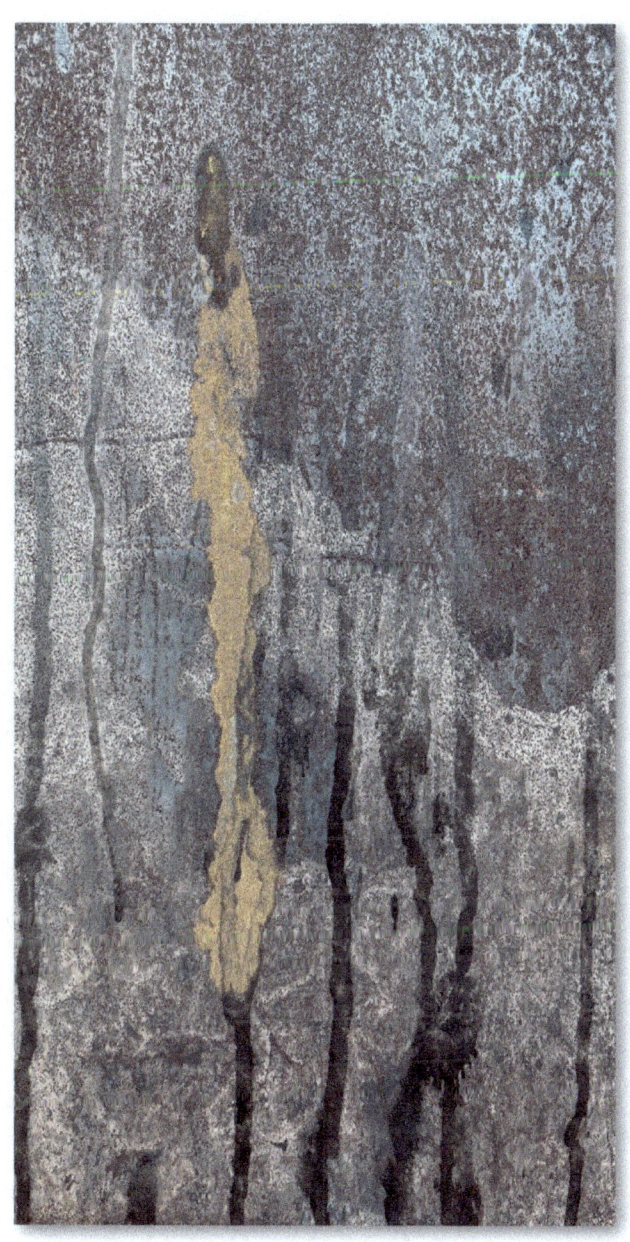

12

SWIMSUIT (2020)

The polka-dot bikini of musical folklore!

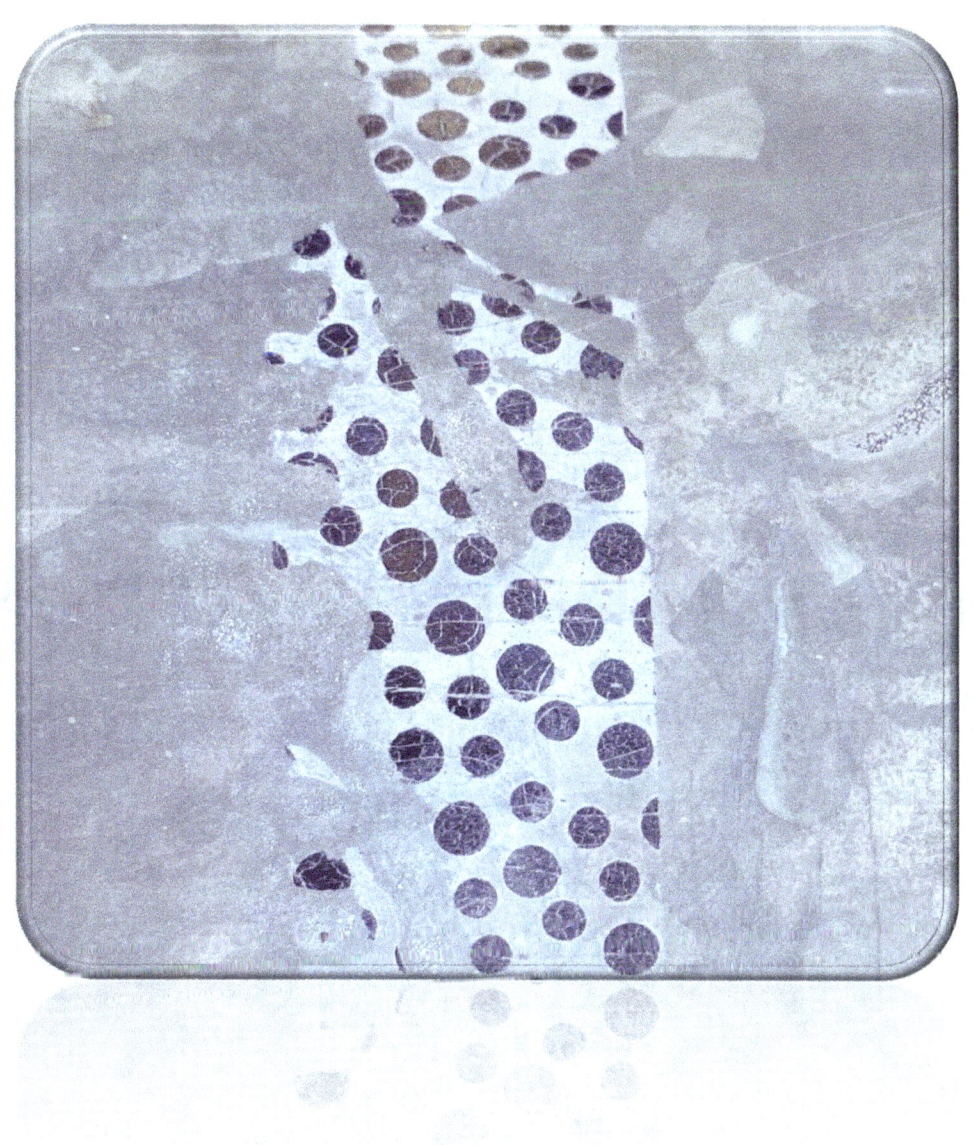

13

DANCE IN REHEARSAL (2015)

Modern interpretive, with a touch of wild.

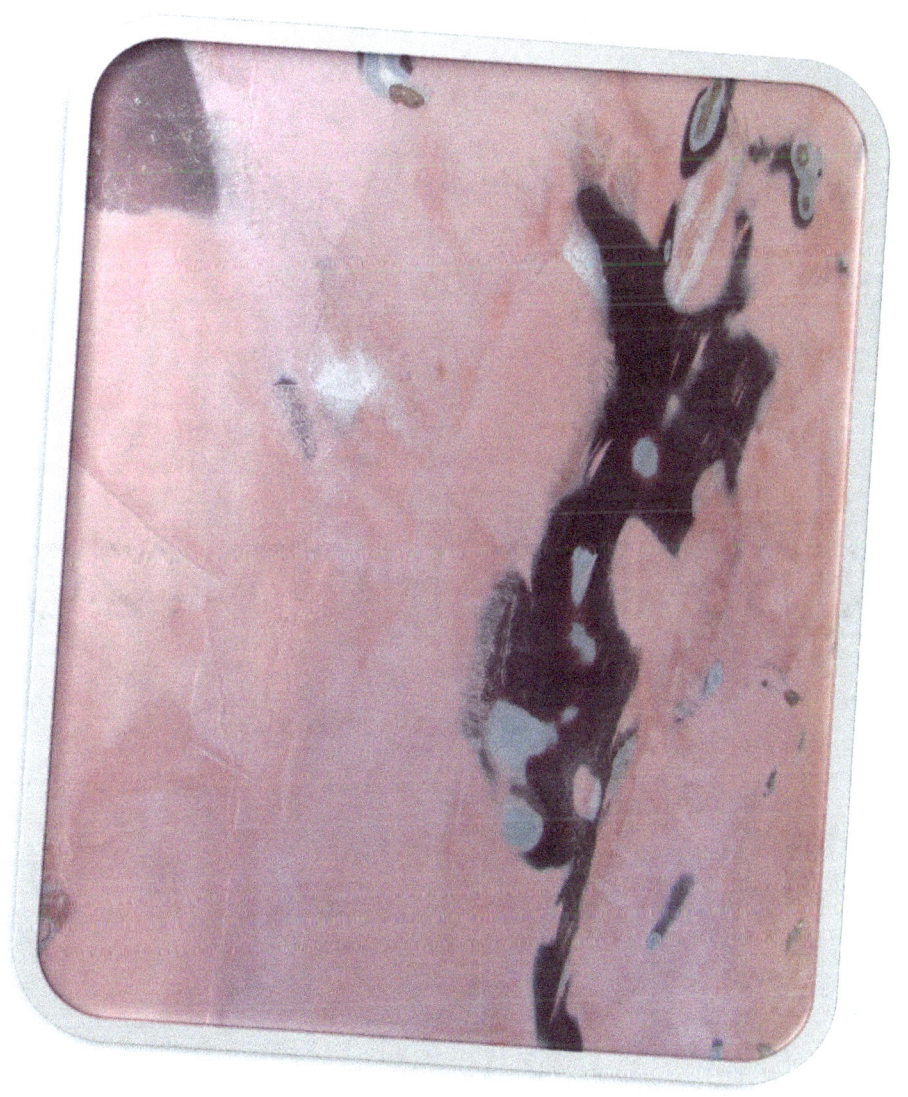

14

KISS ME HOT (2022)

Hello, you fool, I love you [10]

---

10   Roxette, *Joyride,* from the album *Joyride,* 1991.

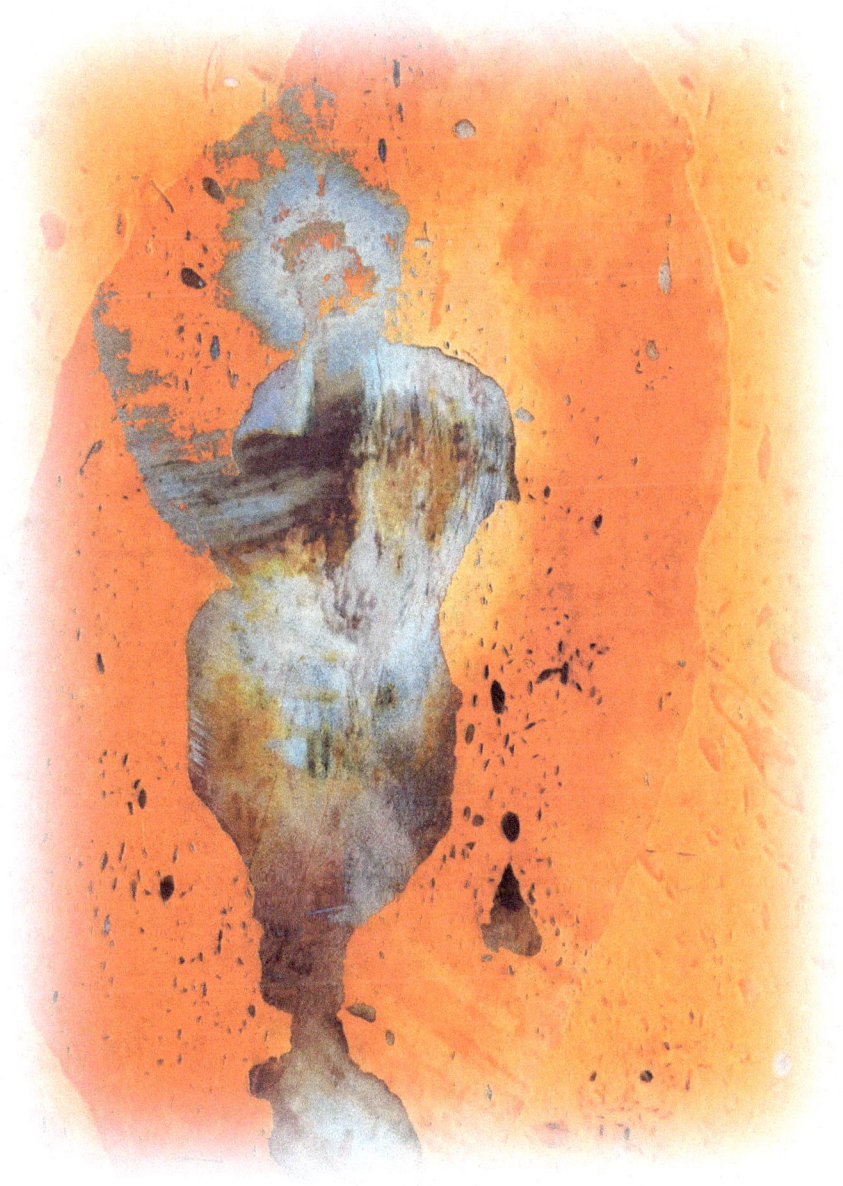

15

WALKIN IN THE 'HOOD (2020)

An inverse of an originally warm-toned pic.

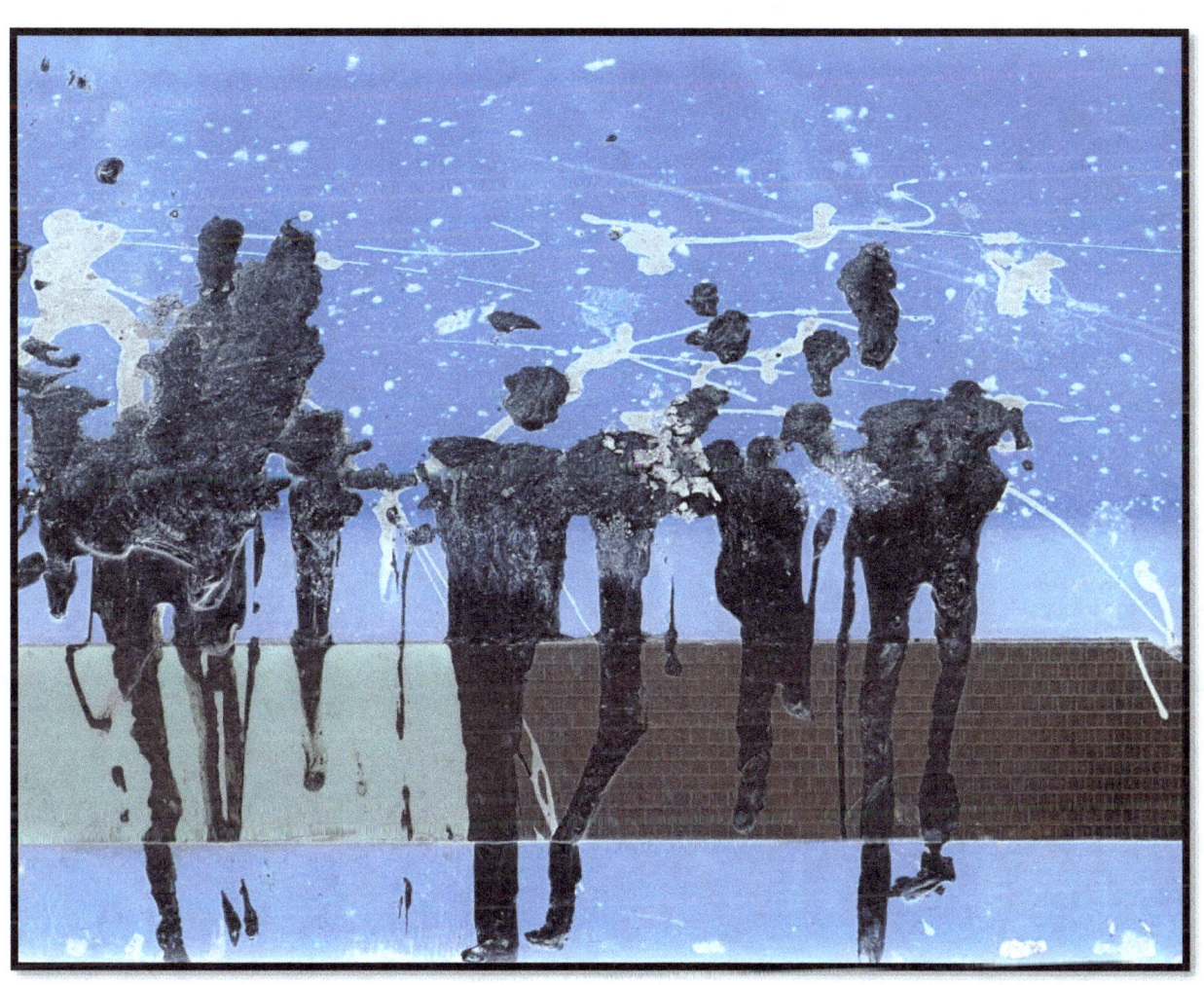

MULTIPLE EXPOSURE

Layer 1.

Layer X.

16

JAPANESE GARDEN W/TREES (2018)

The background is an actual garden.

"Trees" were craquelure images on a wooden wine barrel, which also looks like a linen canvas.

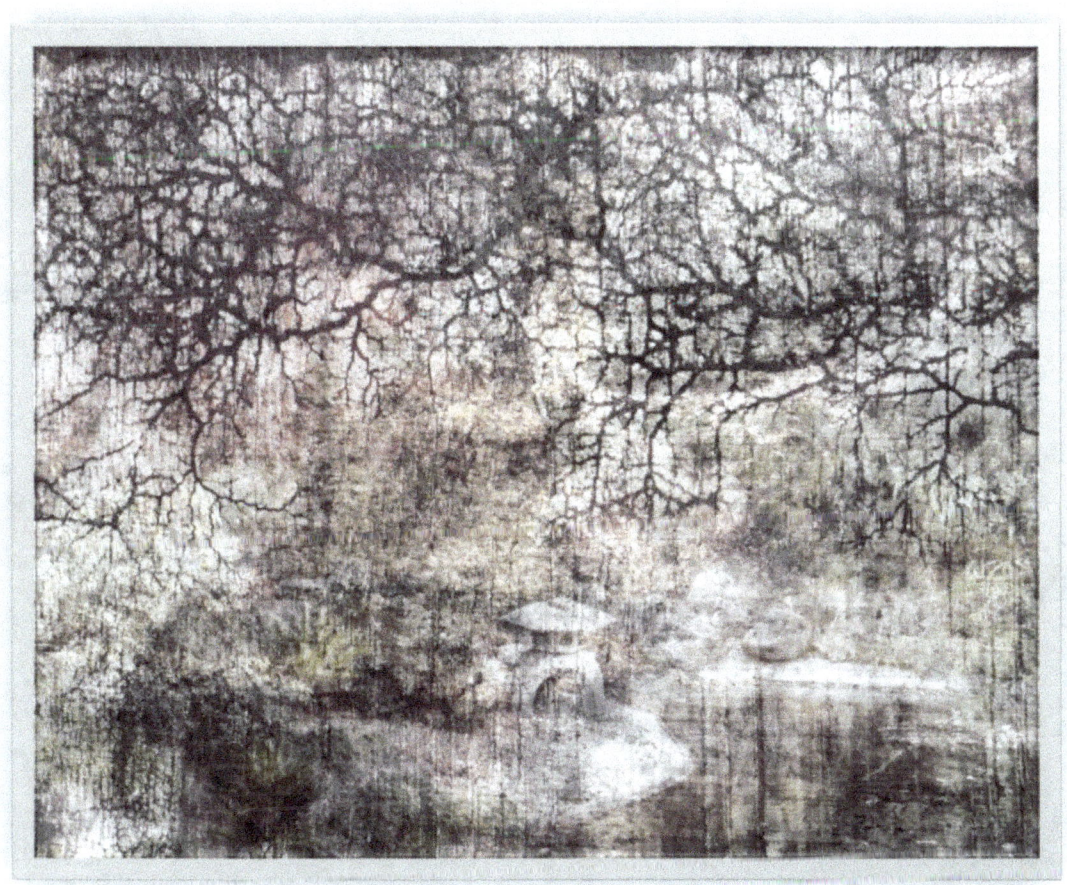

17

COSMIC TRAVEL (2022)

2nd Street Tunnel, Los Angeles CA, with additional overlays.

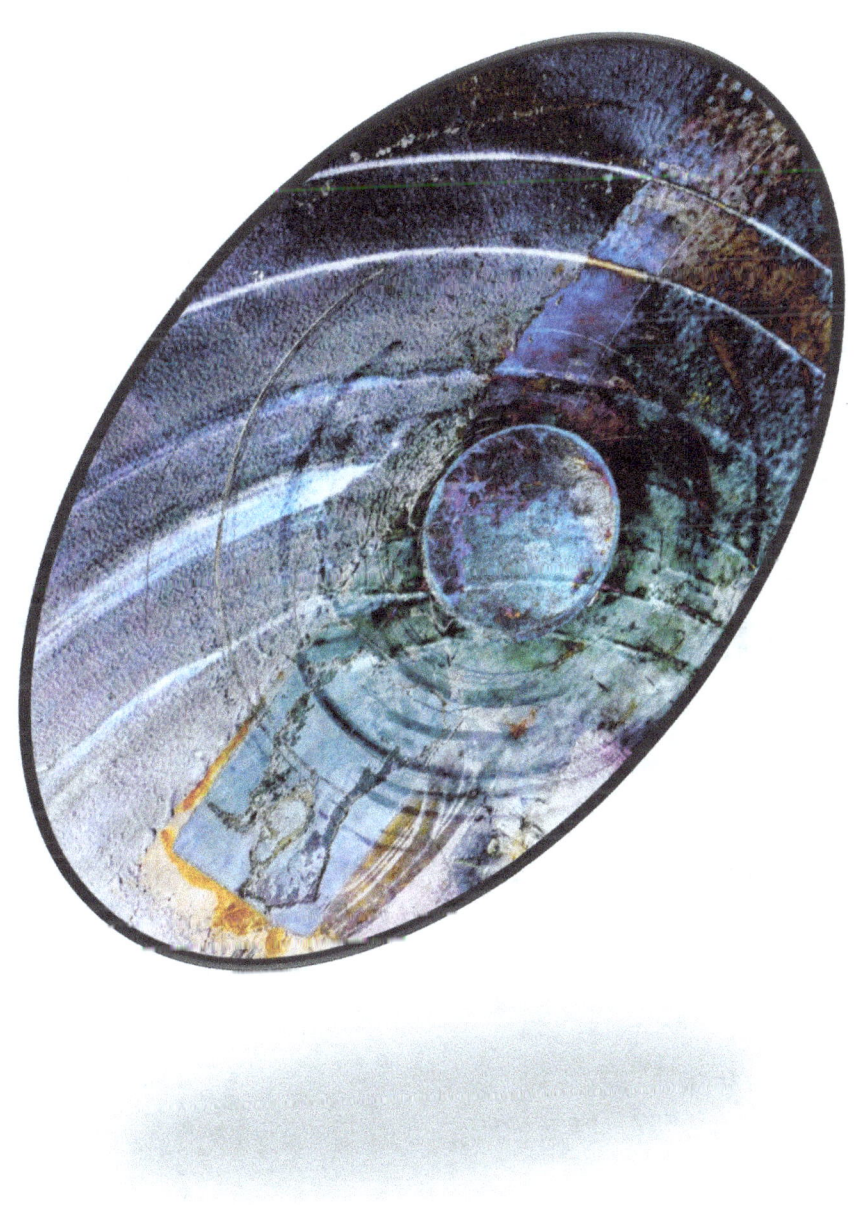

18

COSMIC TUNNEL (2022)

2nd Street Tunnel, Los Angeles, CA, subway tiles, additional overlays.

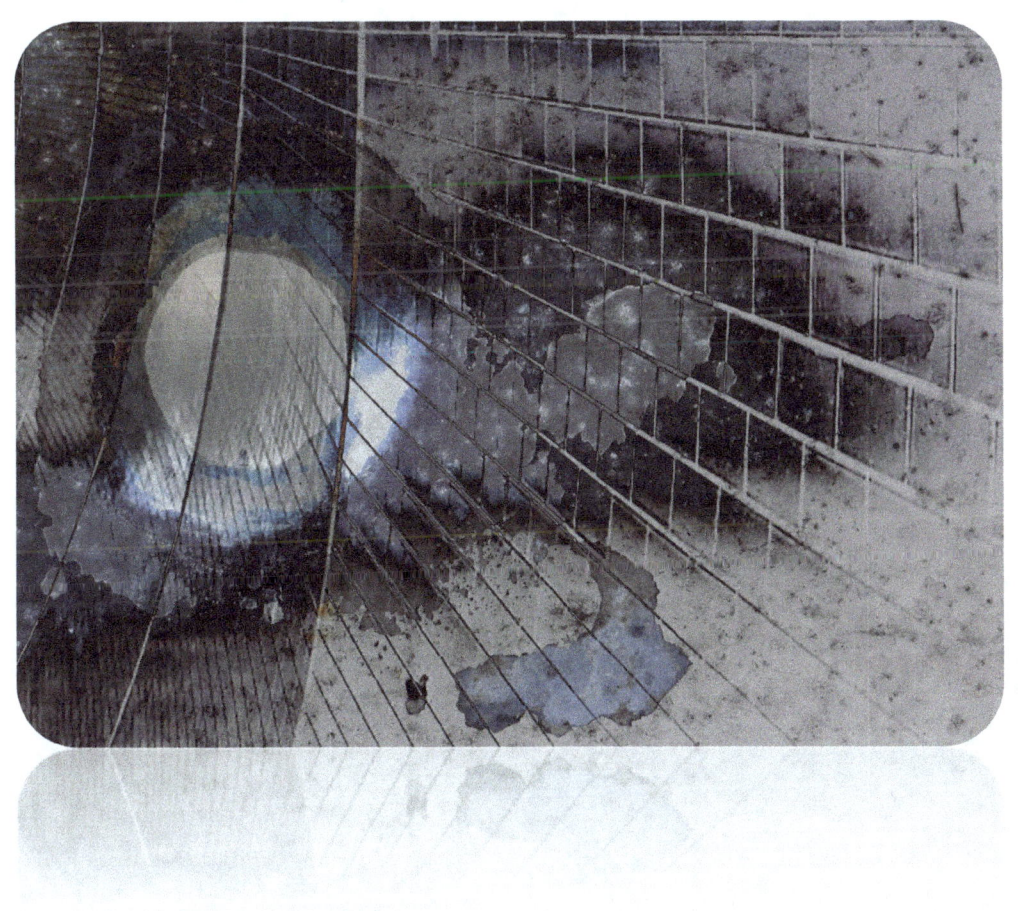

19

WATER HOLE AT EVENING (2019)

Peeling paint from a shipping container with a light color veil.

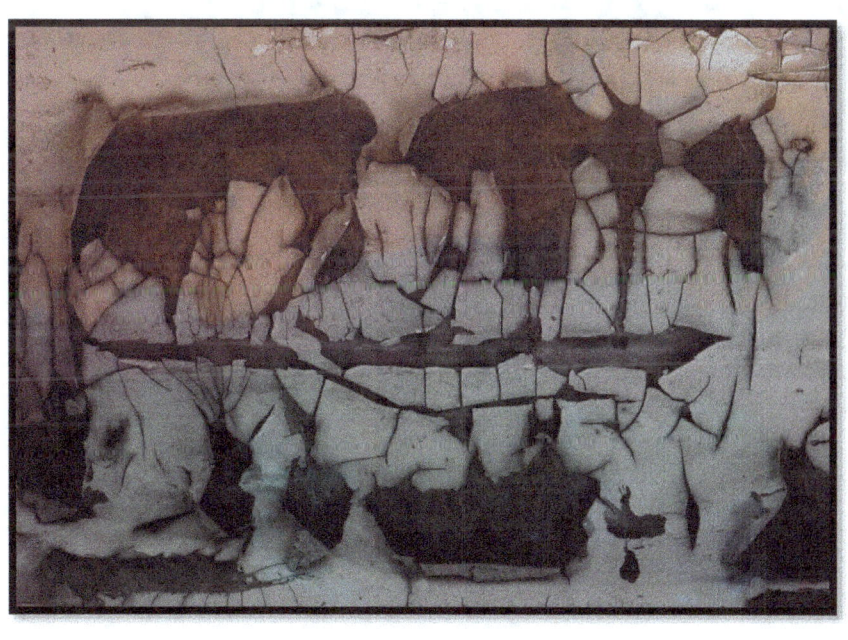

20

WATER HOLE IN HEAT OF AFTERNOON, II (2019)

A warm color palette over the same image.

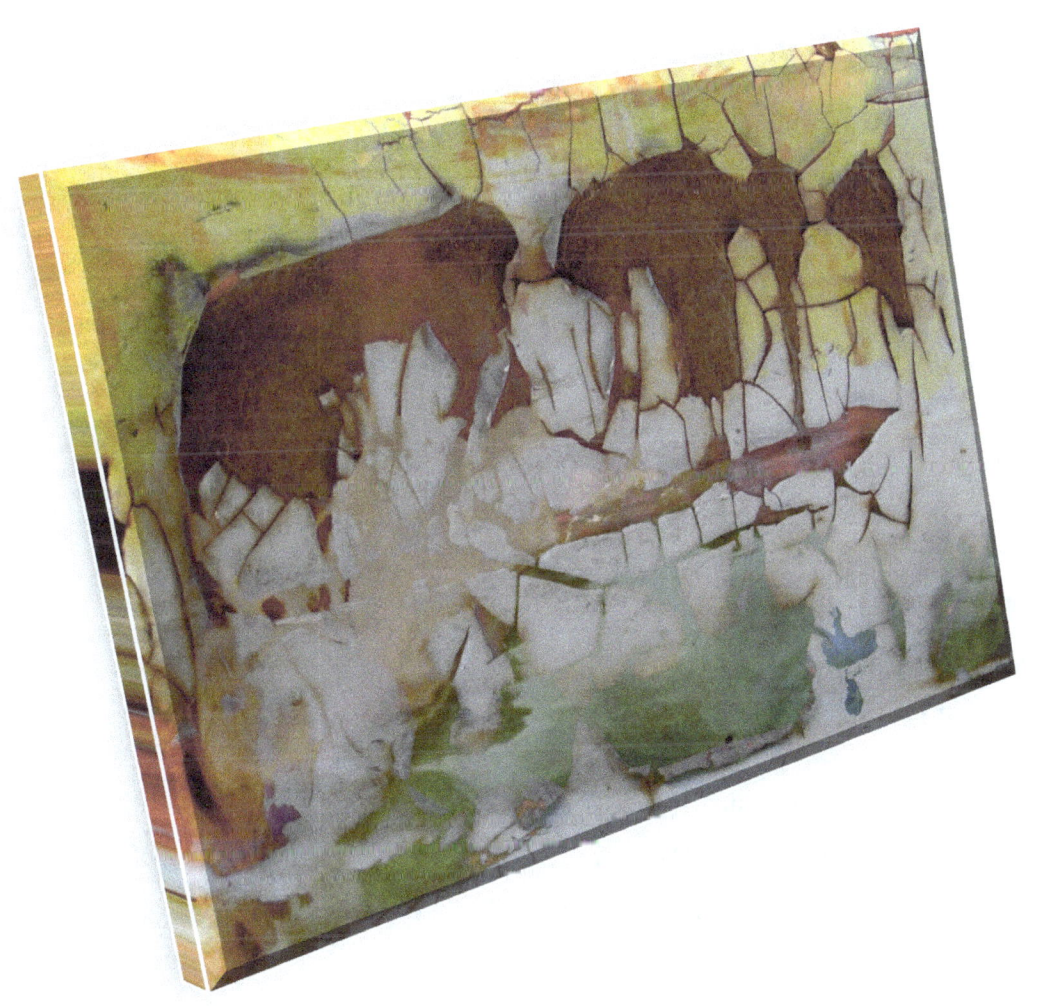

21

COLORS OF MUSIC (2023)

I bought a weird musical instrument from a "freelance street vendor" for its artistic value.

Later learned it's called a ukelin: a two-holed combination of the violin and the Hawaiian ukulele, with zither strings, made popular in the 1920s. Blended its photo with other unrelated shots.

Voila!

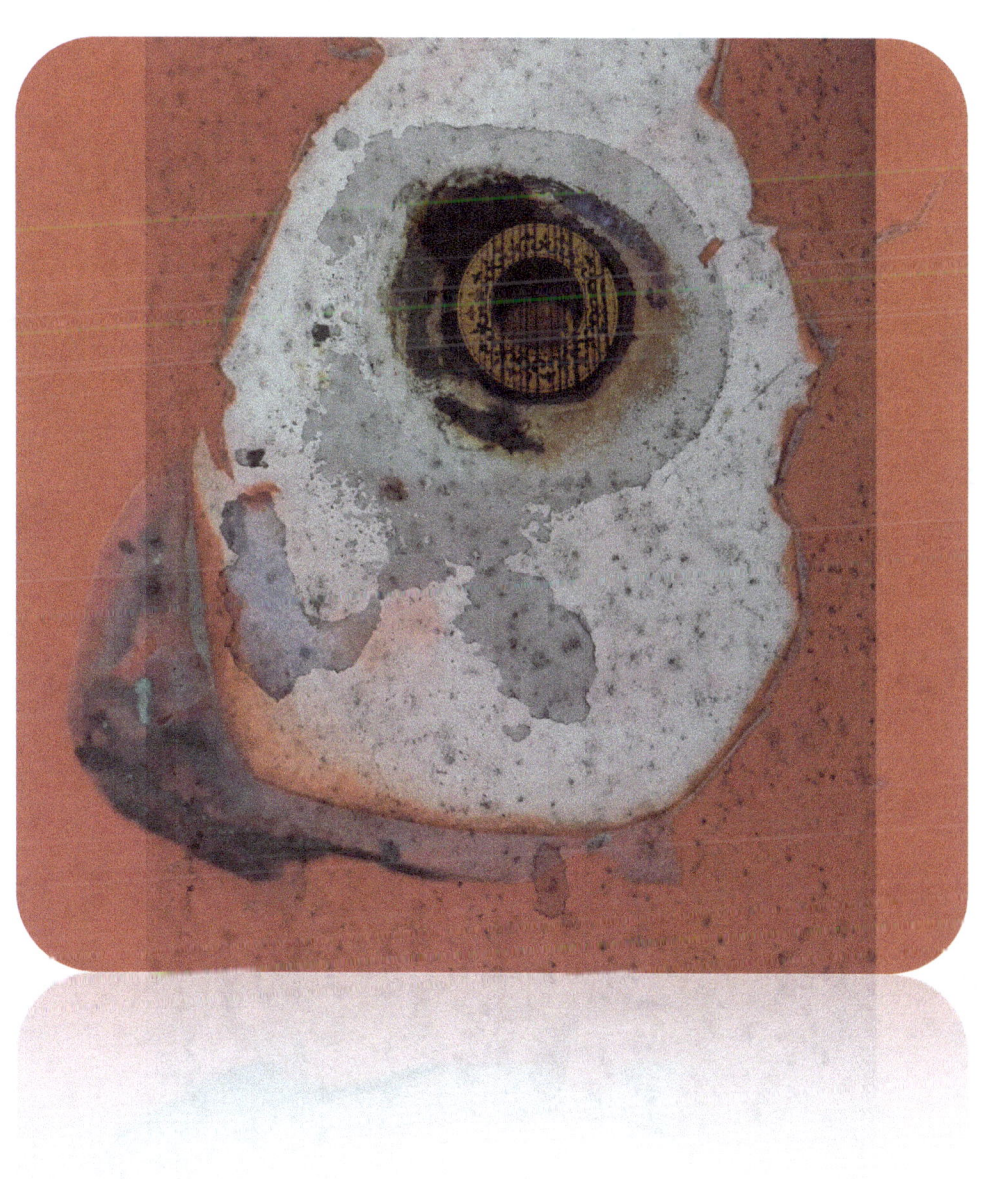

22

GUITARRA (2023)

Ukelin again. Working a series with an element that travels well.

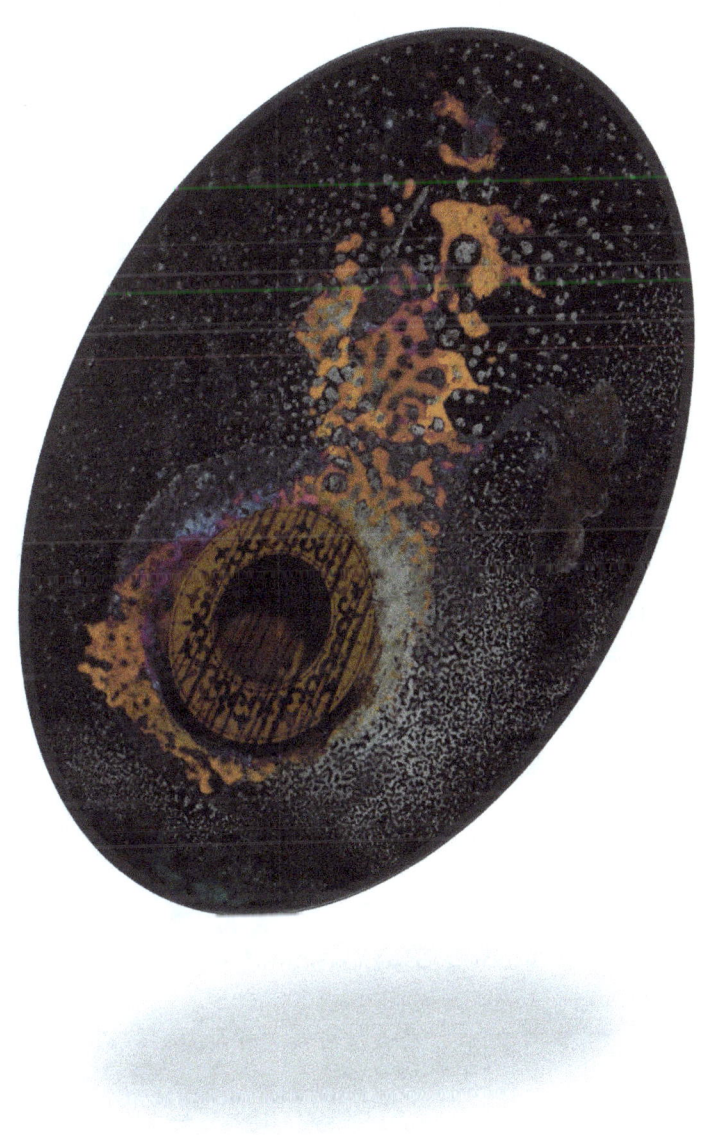

PAINT NOT PAINTING

Yeah, they're paint, but I didn't take up a brush to "paint" anything.

A FIERCE source of contention between photographers and painters, who contend that we photoggs are mechanics, not artists.

We counter with sweeping sarcastic rhetorical questions, asking: what, then, in the wide world is fair game for ANY artist, photographic or otherwise?

Can anything "captured" on film or canvas truly be "original"?

Guaranteed to spoil any cocktail party in 10 minutes flat.

23

UPHILL BOTH WAYS (2021)

Like those preachy stories that Depression-era grandparents tell about walking to school, knee-deep in snow, wearing cereal boxes on their feet, etc. etc. I think the tone of this scene is more thrilling and dangerous.

Lava-filled chasms, a tightrope-precarious ascent, and dire consequences await any misstep.

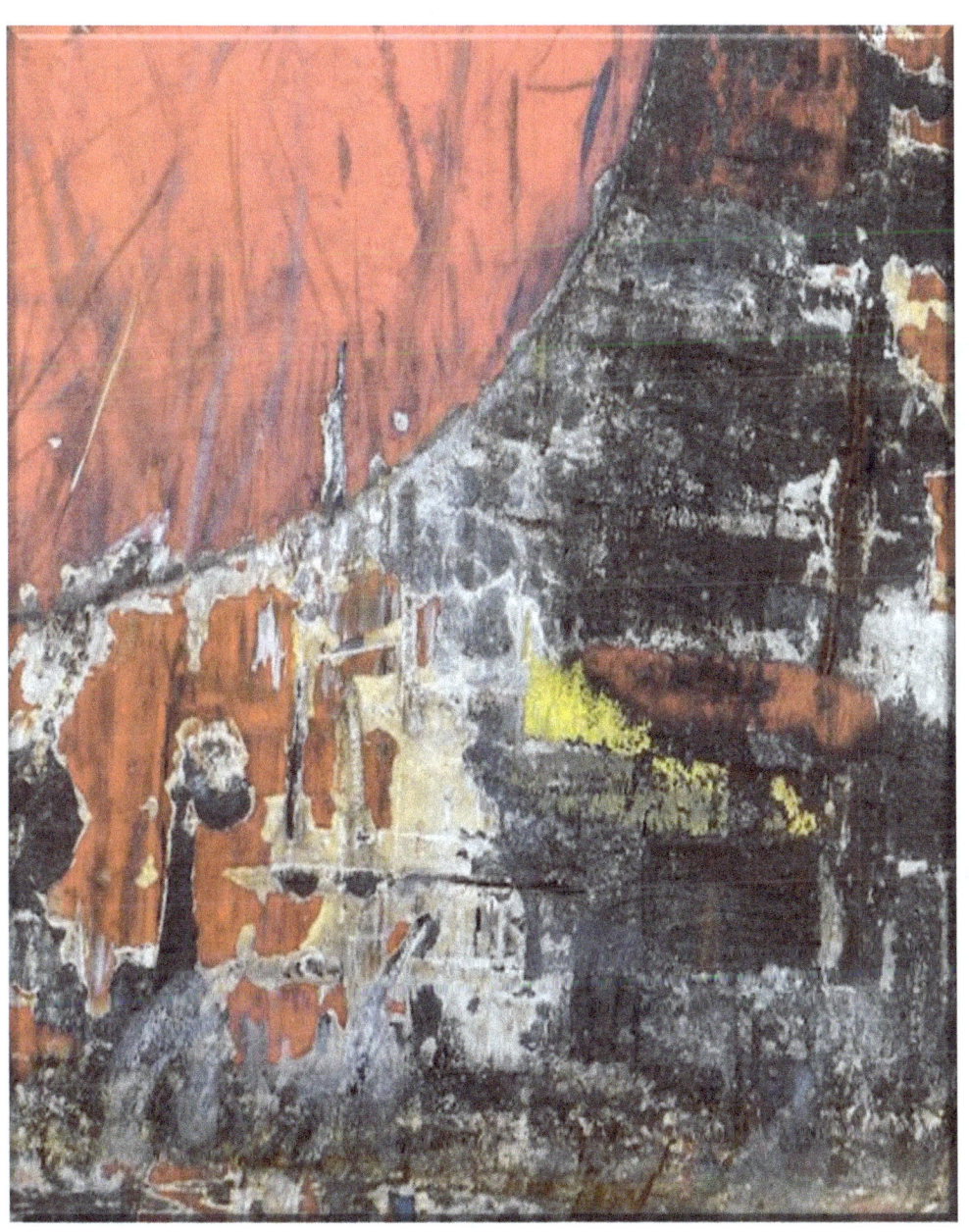

24

BOY AT THE DIKE (2018)

Bricks, water, a kid with a finger stuck in the hole, high drama.

Check, check, check, check!

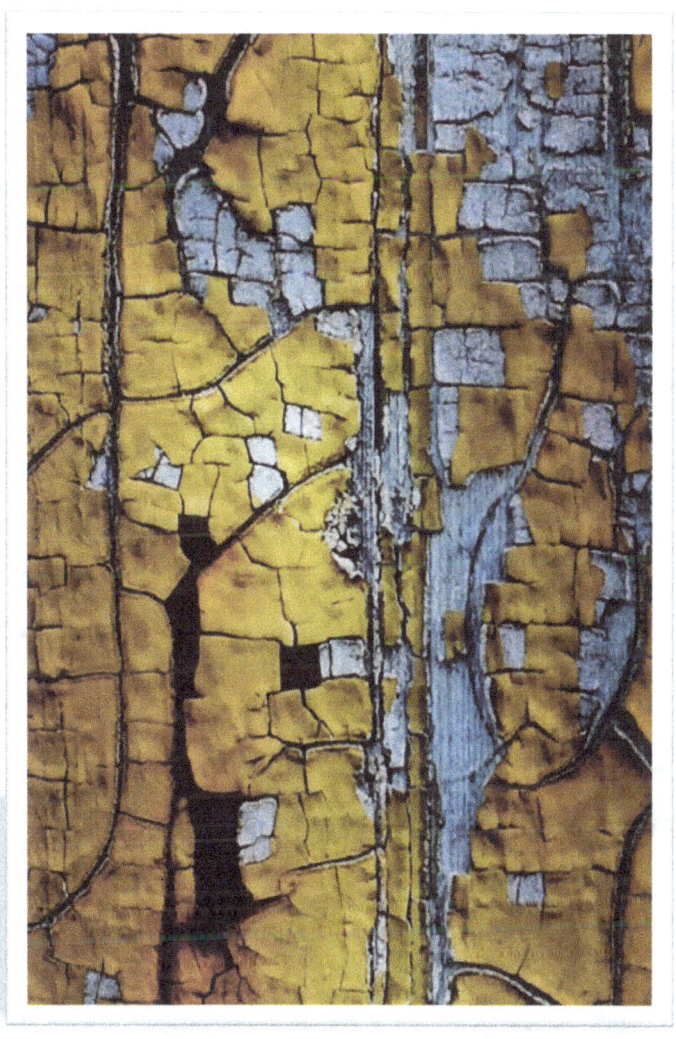

25
NIGHTFALL (2022)

Especially effective when squinting.

Shadow of a cat?

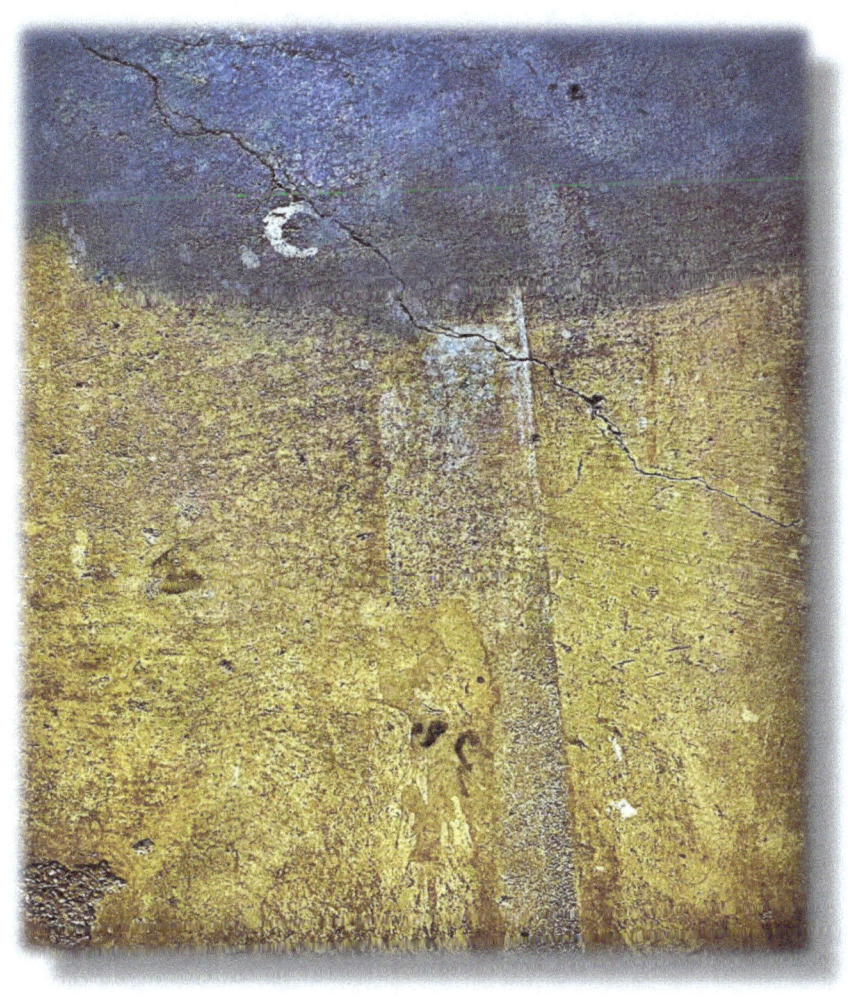

26

THE FISH THAT GOT AWAY (2015)

Where I began my love affair with orbital sanders and power rust removers.

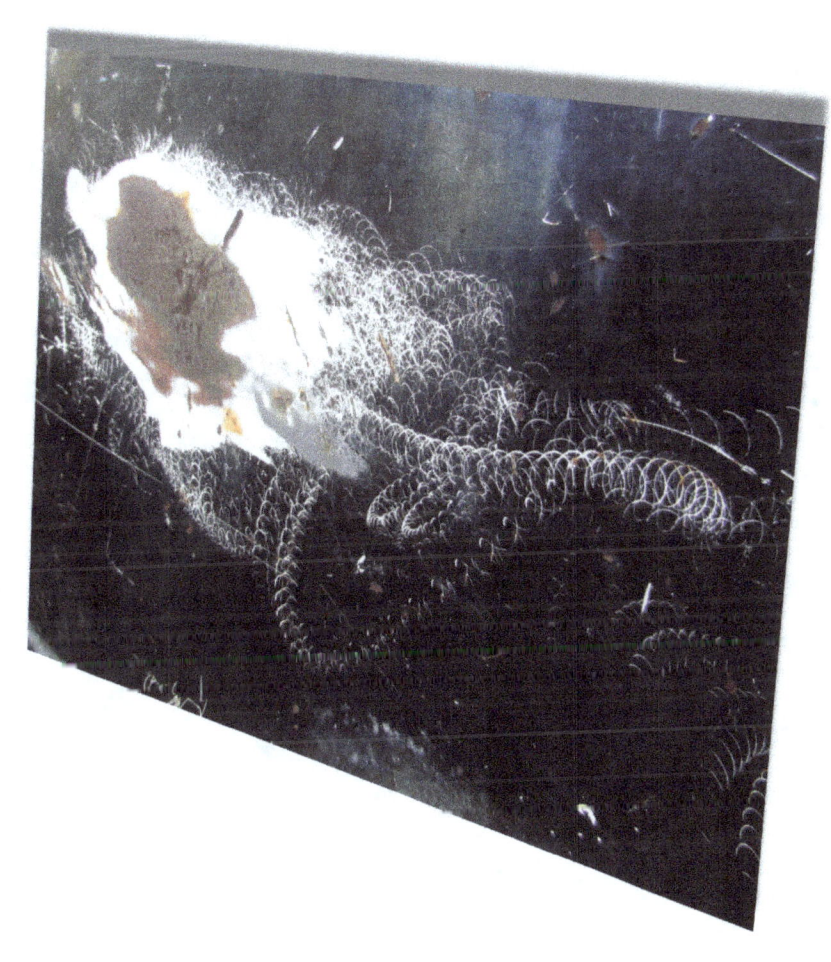

27

KISS ME (2021)

"La Guarachera de Cuba" goddess-singer **Celia Cruz** (shrieking): "Azucar!"

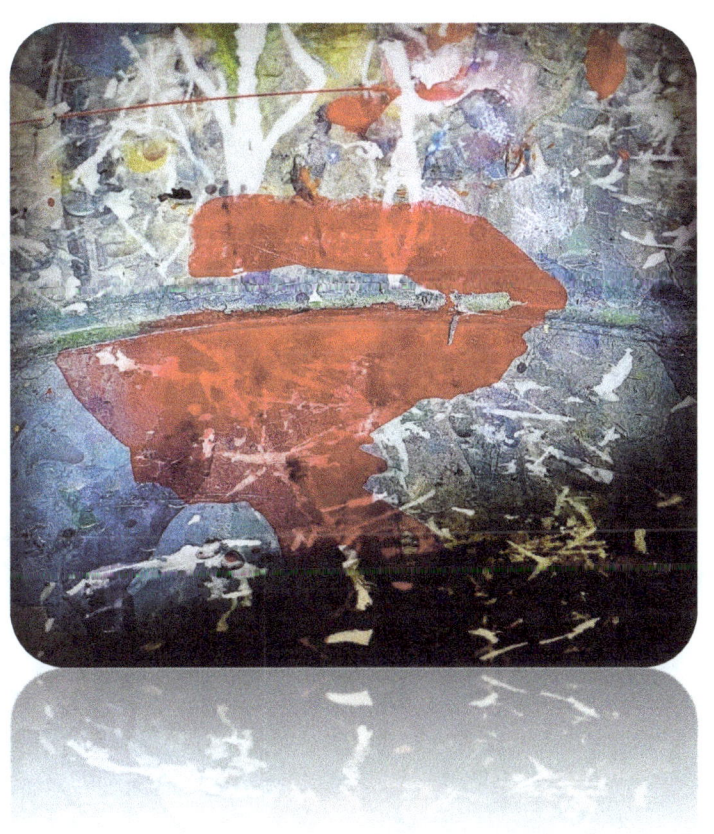

28

SABBATH CANDLE (2020)

Shabbat Shalom.

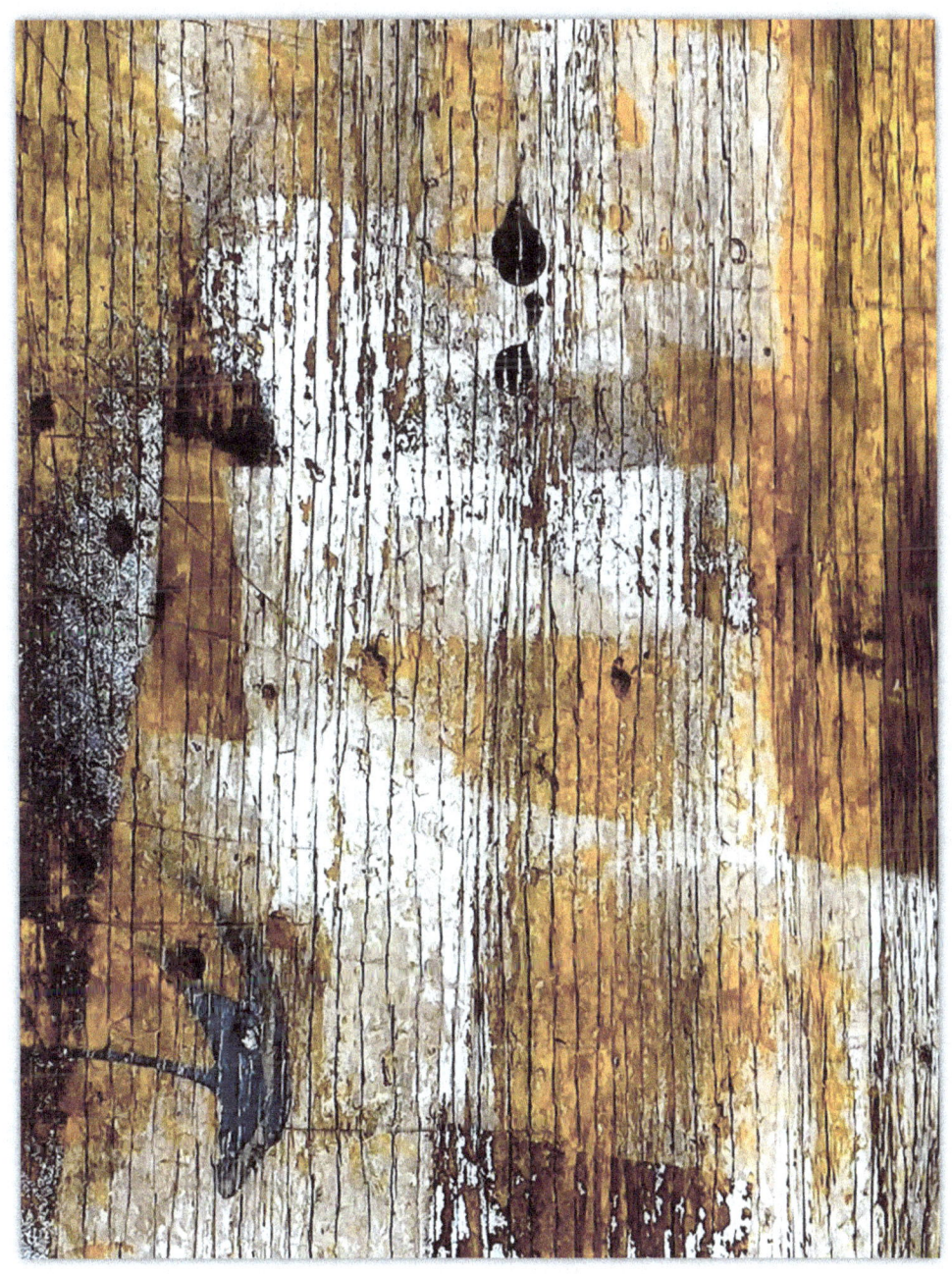

29

CABIN IN THE WOODS (2020)

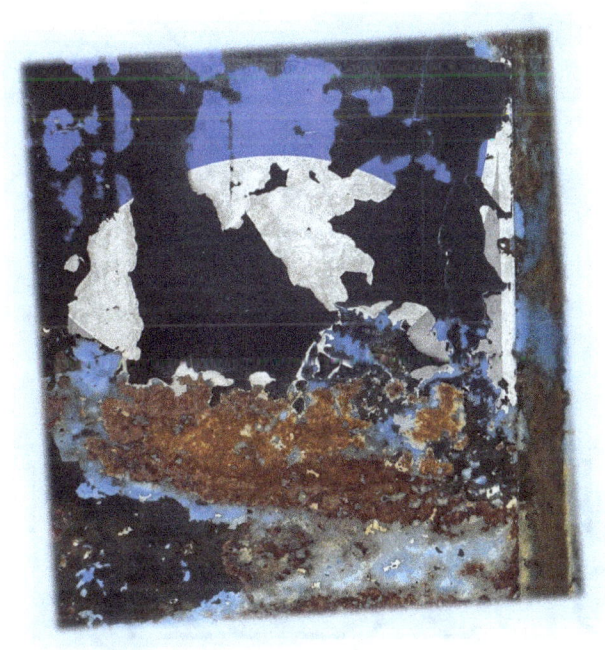

30

WALKING IN WINTER WOODS (2021)

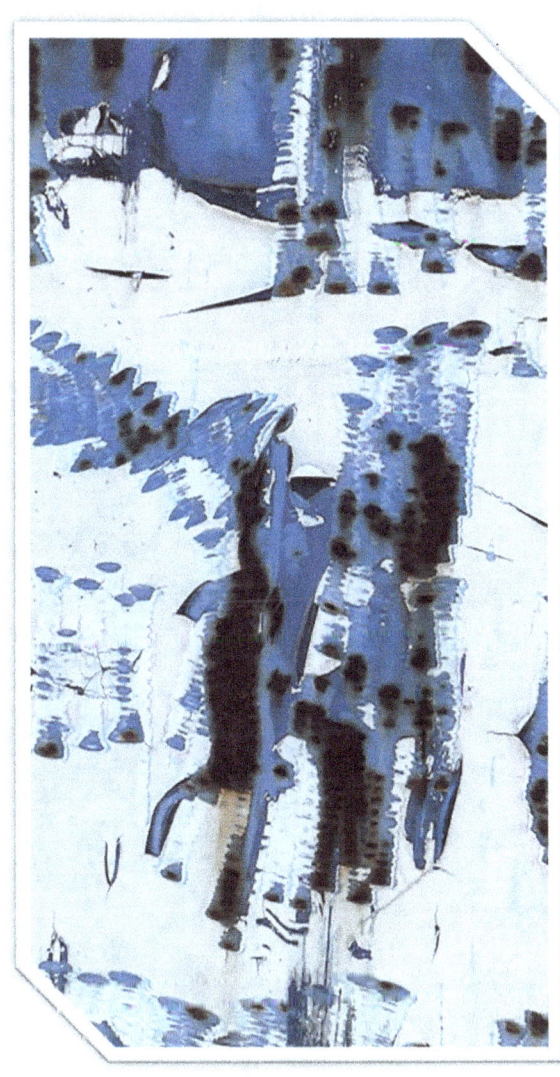

31
SAX (2020)

How about this as a jazz album cover?

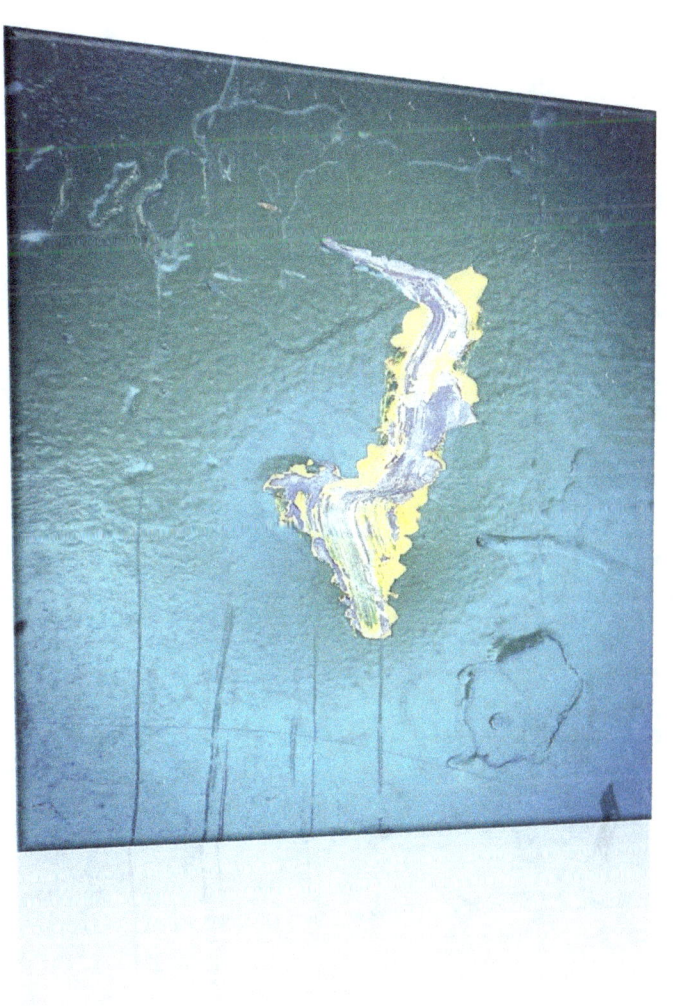

32
FLEDGLING (2017)

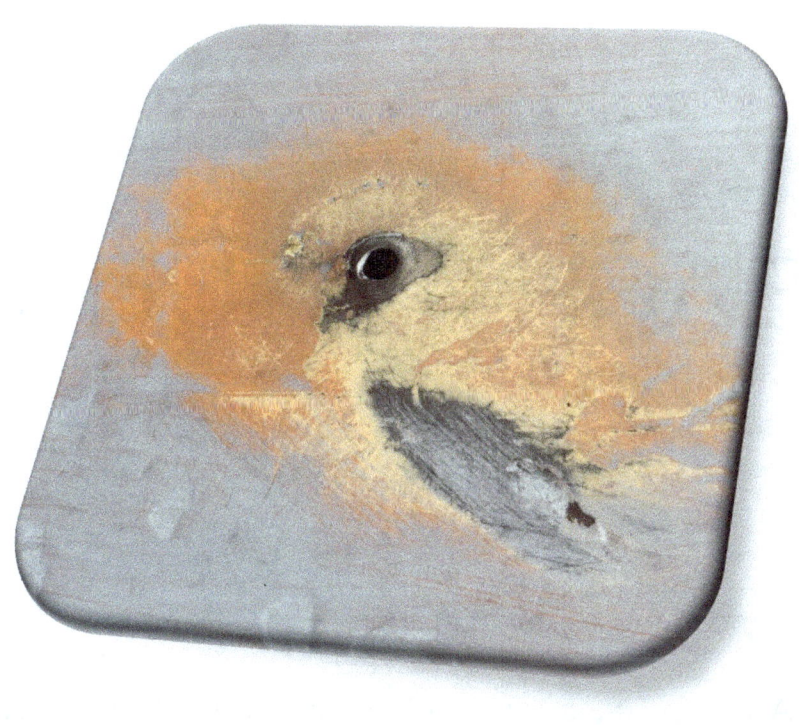

33

BEACH AT SUNSET (2017)

A most unusual source.

A vintage car show, an old Buick with a deeply rusted/pitted/peeled surface.

The owner just sealed it with a half-dozen layers of clear coat finish.

Almost as treasure-ful as a burned dumpster.

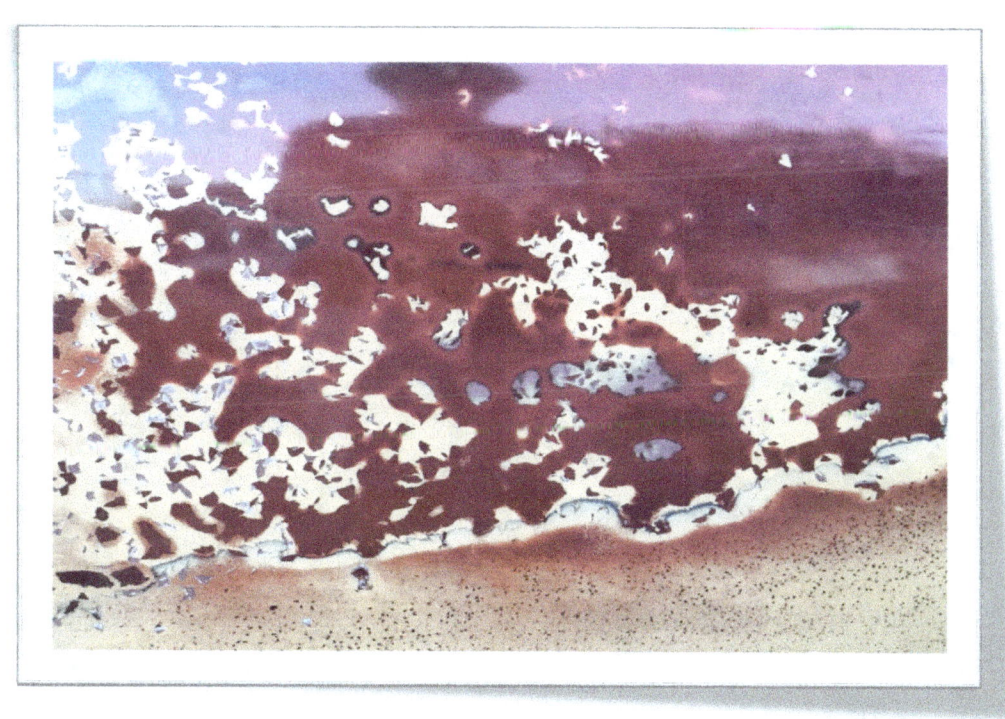

EPILOGUE

[...to the tune of *The Marines' Hymn*]

"From the Dumpsters of New Mexico,
To the shores of Half Moon Bay.
We will shoot our abstract photographs
In the air, on land and sea."

No, it doesn't rhyme.

But it works.

THIS IS ABSTRACTION.

Come join the joyride.

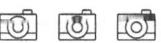

ACKNOWLEDGMENTS

To the Abstract Photographers International [Instagram Tribe]. Our worldwide Zoom meetings are empowering and enlightening. Extra special thanks to J. Alan Constant, Tim Djentle, and Peter Anderson, the founding fathers and administrators; Wendy Kappy (Queen of the New Mexico dumpster artists); Paul Jonathan Rowland & Hintology; Barb Kreutter, ICM magician and layering master; Matthew Fertel and Sierra College (Rocklin, CA); Daryl Burtnett for demo and nudging us to do works in series; and the rest of the energetic gang (see list below and check out their IG pages).

Still and always, Paula Bautista, Paloma Dooley, and Julian Dooley.

Mike Hoover and Vanessa Hadady, mentoring and inspiring even from the other side of the continent.

Shar Marie, and Douglas Feinstein, @sharmarie_studios & @dafoto123, for helping me find a niche and navigate properly on the internet highway.

Jessica Fong, director at the Stockton Art League Goodwin Gallery, for continual encouragement, enthusiasm and brilliant suggestions.

Stacy Sims, for expertise and encouraging artistic experimentation in different mediums.

Kris and Laura Neely, for believing — again!

Evan Freeman, for 24/7 IT support and repair, and for arty conversations about the creative process.

Walt Freeman, for everything everywhere all over the place! Couldn't do it without you, honey!

IG:

Alan Constant @j.alanconstant

Tim Djentle @atimosabe

Peter Anderson @peter_anderson_studio

Wendy Kappy @wendykappyphoto

Paul Rowland (Jonathan Pickles the City) @pauljonathanrowland

Barb Kreutter @barbkreutter

Matthew Fertel @digprod4

Daryl Burtnett @darylburtnett

Lorne Fromer @lornefromer_flaneur

Josh Feldman @cooperedtot

Muriel Gani @murielgani

Nirvana SQ @nirvana_s_q

Anke @frau_kraut

Jess Heard @visuals4cacophony

BIOGRAPHY

Annie Mack (*b. Anne McCaughey*) is an art photographer and retired teacher based in Northern California.

Her first book, *Badass Pix with a Cheap-Ass Camera*, also published by Cresting Wave Publishing, is a treatise and portfolio on non-traditional approaches to photography. Her photo collage work was a prize winner in the 2015 *Dave Brubeck Jazz Festival* of the University of the Pacific, and she has won awards in traditional photography and mixed media.

She is an active member of Abstract Photographers International — a group of online abstractionists in North America, Europe, and Japan. Her work has appeared in Hintology Magazine, and she is currently teaching online courses on developing artistic creativity.

Notes

Notes

www.ingramcontent.com/pod-product-compliance
Lightning Source LLC
Chambersburg PA
CBHW081732220526

45468CB00008B/2068